TROPICAL PARADISE
©2000 Page One Publishing Pte Ltd
Published by HBI, an Imprint of HarperCollins Publishers
and Watson-Guptill Publishers

Distributed in the U.S. and Canada by
Watson-Guptill Publications
1515 Broadway
New York, NY 10036
Tel: (800) 451-1741
Tel: (732) 363-4511 in NJ, AK, HI
Fax: (732) 363-0338
ISBN: 0-8230-5451-9

Distributed worldwide (excluding Southeast Asia & Australia) by
HarperCollins International
10 East 53rd Street
New York, NY 10022-5299
Fax: (212) 207-7654
ISBN: 0688-17269-5

Distributed in Southeast Asia & Australia by
Page One The Bookshop Pte Ltd
20 Kaki Bukit View, Kaki Bukit Techpark II
Singapore 415956
Tel: (65) 742-2088
Fax: (65) 744-2088
Email: pageone@singnet.com.sg
ISBN: 981-4019-03-8

Design : Creative In-House Limited and Bensley Design Studios, Bangkok
Colour separation : Singapore Sang Choy Colour Separation Pte Ltd
Production : Maxim Design Consultants, Singapore
Printed and bound : CS Graphics Pte Ltd, Singapore

"To you, to me, Stonehenge and Chartres Cathedral … are works by the same Old Man under different names: we know what He did, what, even, He thought He thought, but we don't see why."

W. H. Auden

TROPICAL PARADISE

TAN HOCK BENG

PHOTOGRAPHS BY BILL BENSLEY

HBI, an Imprint of HarperCollins Publishers

Watson-Guptill Publishers

THE TOURIST
LANDSCAPE
IN ASIA

Tropical Asia is one of the culturally richest regions in the world. It also has exceptional landscapes and stunning natural features - factors that made the region a major tourist destination. Except for a brief hiccup during the economic crisis of the late 90's, the region has experienced tremendous growth in the construction of new hotels and resorts.

Tropical Asia

is one of the culturally richest regions in the world. It also has exceptional landscapes and stunning natural features – factors that made the region a major tourist destination. Except for a brief hiccup during the economic crisis of the late 90's, the region has experienced tremendous growth in the construction of new hotels and resorts.

The collection of highly tactile works in this volume is the product of an intense collaboration between the landscape practice of Bensley Design Studios and the architectural practice of Bunnag Architects. Based in Bangkok, the two designers, and in particular, the principals - Bill Bensley and Mathar 'Lek' Bunnag - have crafted syntheses of landscape and buildings of simple materiality, consummate craftsmanship and rich moods. Many of these exclusive enclaves offer an intriguing subject for critics and cultural theorists. The buildings are unconventional, and are approached with inventive imagination. Inspired by a reverence for the tropical climate, the rich cultural heritage as well as the usually pristine sites, the buildings demonstrate a poetic understanding and keen appreciation of the phenomenal and cultural worlds.

The designers' sensitivities to climatic and cultural determinants, as well as their awareness of working in a specific spatial and temporal environment, are highly obvious. Their combined plethora of multi-referential architecture and landscape, with their tactile corporeality, emphasizes the inherent beguiling qualities of truly tropical design with a meticulous zeal that is rare.

Showcasing a prolific range of invigorating works that is meticulously executed, the book also incorporates many of the inimitable presentation techniques of the two practices. It hopes to convey the sensual refinement and expressive potency of qualities found in the projects - like humor, deception, surprise and drama - that all add up to the poetics of built forms in Tropical Asia. Threatened by the forces of universal commodification, these enticing works grew out of a poetic and allegorical way of thinking. They are truly a subtle blend of landscape and architecture - of empathy and resonance - one that grounds their inhabitants and visitors in the specificity and poetics of place.

Arguably, the trailblazer of the resort scene in Asia during the late 1980's was the pioneering series of "exclusive private-villas resorts". Many of these expensive properties, located in sumptuous surroundings, have been nothing less than phenomenal. In many ways, they have re-defined the philosophy of resort creation.

Below: *A row of variegated dwarf bamboo forms the edge of the spiky plants garden at Kandawgyi Palace Hotel in Yangon, Myanmar.*
Opposite: *A plate of dried chillies serves as an interesting accent piece at a garden gazebo at the Novotel Lombok.*

Architecturally, these properties stand out for their ongoing pursuit of functionalism infused with Asian essence, committed as much to modernity as to local culture. The juxtaposition of current fashion trends, like minimalism, and abstracted elements of traditional design, has resulted in a particular style that has appeals both globally as well as at the local levels. For the jet-setting tourist or journalist, these resorts look reassuringly familiar, yet exotic. Hence, the term "hip" has sometimes been used to describe these ultra-chic resorts.

Anthropologically, they reflect the increasingly deep interest of the world's travelling middle class, who go to the host countries "experiencing" and pursuing proofs of their "authentic" contact with exotic cultures. In our vicarious, media-driven cultures, touristic consciousness is motivated by the desire for experiencing "authenticity" in "back-stage" regions. This quest for authenticity has undoubtedly spawned a series of resorts that claimed to be authentic interpretations of traditional architecture of the respective regions.

In this age of unconstrained mobility, the most rapidly developing tourism region globally has been East Asia and the Pacific area, whose rapid econom-

ic development, until the onset of the economic crisis in 1997, has stimulated travel of an unprecedented scale.

The leisure-makers of Asia often use traditions and heritage, both authentic and manufactured, for mass consumption. The tourism industry has thus successfully constructed a new niche by marketing the concept of authenticity which offer tourists a more "culturally sensitive" and "politically correct" form of travel accommodation. The design of these "impossible-to-reach hideaways" is essentially a calculated conflation of nostalgia-marketing and manufactured traditions. Architecture thus becomes an important part of this experience.

With the widespread popularity of minimalism in architecture and interior design, many of these resorts adopt a similar "Less Is More" stylistic approach. Many of them become trendy, hip hotspots for the fashion-mongers. The more successful ones are able to blend the local with the universal, hence appealing to a wide spectrum of guests. Designers mix ideas and influences from near and far - combining the existing with the imported – and in the process, create exciting and refreshing concoctions of hybridized designs.

As a result, a wide spectrum of hotels and resorts are being built at a mind-boggling pace and scale, seeming to double their numbers with every blink of the eye. Well-worn tourist spots like Bali and Phuket, as well as prospective regions like Krabi in Thailand, Indonesia's Bintan, Manado in Sulawesi and Lampung in Sumatra, are earmarked for extensive development in order to attract the growing share of tourists. Bali, "Island of the Gods", remains an unfailingly attractive tourist destination. It plays a major role in Indonesia's tourism industry which brings in more than US$3 billion (S$4.5 billion) a year from foreign exchange.

In such an increasingly competitive environment, resort design is constantly in a process of evolution. Recent trends indicate that resorts are beginning to specialize in niche marketing. The highly differentiated market now includes time-sharing resorts, health and spa resorts, condo hotels, suite hotels, boutique resorts and vacation villages. These range from mega-resorts like the Laguna Resort in Phuket and the 750-room Grand Hyatt Bali, to exclusive deluxe resorts designed as "boutique resorts".

Many players heralded the concept of "lifestyle resorts" which seek to evoke a touristic lifestyle that is fashionably hip, culturally authentic and architecturally exciting. Spas are becoming important mainstays of these lifestyle resorts. With the trend towards healthy living, spas are becoming a major attraction for many "hip" tourists. These new destinations, like the Regent Spa in Chiang Mai, besides providing a luxurious backdrop for spa activities, also amplify the sensual qualities that complement the whole ritual of going to a spa. These ineffably sensual buildings, with their strong emphasis on the tactility and materiality of local building cultures, will almost certainly acquire cult status.

Architects of these stylish works have produced an architectural ensemble that possesses a sensual refinement and a sure sense of place. The concept of luxury is re-defined through a sense of tactility and tranquility. Exclusivity and sensuality are key words to describe many of these sybaritic and stimulating havens.

The best of these building types possess levels of sophistica-tion and quality that other trite hotels clear-l y lack.

Materials are used in a manner that delights while the spatial effects created are a pleasure to experience. The prolific range of works by Mathar "Lek" Bunnag and Bill Bensley has added greatly to the current stock of projects in this genre.

Based in Bangkok and Bali, both are ideally situated in the "eye of the storm" – where they are able to tap into the rich cultural veins of Thailand and Indonesia simultaneously. Bunnag himself is acutely sensitive to the cultural complexities of Southeast Asia. His Harvard graduate thesis, "Conservation of Meaning", received distinction from the University, and reflects his long-standing interest in architectural projects that embody cultural heritage. "For me," Bunnag reiter-ates, " respect and appreciation of the Thai cultural heritage has helped me to understand other cultures better. This is especially so in Southeast Asia, where our cultural ties are strong. I feel that I am using Thai culture as a lens to appreciate and understand other cultural heritage." Together with Bensley, the pair has col-laborated on many resorts in Asia.

Both went to graduate school together, and upon gradu-a t i o n ,

B u n n a g t a u g h t briefly a t

the School of Architecture, National University of Singapore, while Bensley worked for an American landscape architecture firm in Singapore and Hong Kong for five years. Both came to Bangkok in 1989 to set up a shared studio comprising some fifty artists, artisans and designers. Bensley further maintains another studio in Bali. There is an obvious enthrallment with the crafted and the handmade. As Bensley argues: " Our studios are different from many because there is a shared passion for the Arts, and a keen pursuit of Beauty in all forms. "

An acknowledged maestro of resort landscaping in Asia, Bensley has created a memorable series of places and experiences, imbued with brilliant flashes of wit and elegance. In his restless quest for beauty in tropical gardens, Bensley attempts to create an environment of ambivalent qualities, managing to be very natural and yet somehow very contrived simultaneously. By juxtaposing calculated abandon with manmade whimsy and irreverence, he gives these gardens a sense of relative significance.

Lek Bunnag's architecture, on the other hand, is planned with much delicacy and meticulous

zeal. His works, drawing strongly on the vernacular of the particular regions, introduce tactile gratification and a precious sense of the tectonic. Some critics describe his works as being obsessively elaborate. Indeed, they are invariably multi-faceted, enticing, and at the same time, provocative. Bensley's willful sculpting of the land has an empathy and resonance with Bunnag's poignant buildings. In the search for meaning within architectural form and landscape, the resultant works are eminently suited to their respective sites.

This tender appreciation of both the phenomenal and cultural landscapes throws up a series of questions on the issues of modernity and tradition, replication and reinvention – issues that continually challenge and confront all architects practicing in Asia.

In any case, critics have always question the validity of resorts - seen as enclaves of pleasure - in the Third World environment where there are more pressing architectural issues like resettlement and rural planning. Furthermore, the architecture of tourism usually destroys that which the tourist has come to experience. However, this should not hinder us from acknowledging the fact that outstanding ones steer clear from the superficial gimmicks, piped culture and vulgar display of paper-thin forms.

Although these unabashedly hedonistic settings cannot claim to have tackled social issues, they do promote greater public awareness of the rich vernacular heritage. They are also an important source of inspiration for many subsequent local works. Many recent detached houses designed in Southeast Asia, in particular, are greatly influenced by the architecture of these resorts in Thailand and Indonesia.

The task is to create architecture that is not only sensually engaging, but which is also a combination of sensitive re-interpretations of the past and innovative use of local skills and

materials. Bensley and Bunnag's works, executed as a complementary endeavor, evidently demonstrate that both architects positively relish these issues.

9

INSPIRATION

"SOURCES AND IMAGERY"

"Beauty speaks like an oracle, and ever since, man has heeded its message in an infinite number of ways … Human life deprived of beauty is not worthy of being called so."

Luis Barragan

Pesamuan Bali

As post-industrial civilization seeks to reduce the world to one vast commodity, and as the world becomes more globalized, art forms inevitably become intermingled. In the face of the transcending power of the media, the role of architecture in place making and in the evocation of traditions has been questioned.

Yet, despite the perceived homogenization, the use of cultural specificity is in no way less vigorous. Manuel Castells suggests that against the normative trend of computer-networked world, "local societies, territorially defined, must preserve their identities, and build on their historical roots, regardless of their economic and functional dependence upon the space of flows".

In the context of Asia, it has become quite apparent that many designers are pursuing an engagement with traditions and specifics of locality with renewed vigor during the last decade. This pursuit of tradition is in many ways exacerbated by the phenomenon of tourism. Modern mass tourism has important social consequences. It is based on two contradictory phenomena: on the one hand, a global homogenization of the culture of the tourists, and on the other, the preservation of local ethnic groups and attractions for touristic consumption.

Any built environment inevitably reflects the constructed expression of culture and history. The acts of seeing and experiencing the environment assail all the senses. This is further heightened when one experiences a totally new environment, especially when visiting a foreign country. Away from the pressures of everyday life, one experiences unfamiliar environments in a more relaxed, and hence "hypersensitive" manner. With such a mindset, the act of inspiration becomes spontaneous.easy.

Inspiration involves observing and participating fully in the environment. At the same time, inspiration has to do with appreciating the purpose of the design elements one encounter and understanding why they evoke such admiration. The desire to translate such inspirational elements into new works is natural.

Above and below: Elaborate tapestry and strong colors can be found in most traditional Asian costumes. They are a rich source of inspiration as well. **Page 15 Top left:** *A polished plaster wall decoration found in an ancient palace in the city Palace of Udaipur, India.* **Top middle:** *A pair of painted eyes on a Nepali Chedi structure.* **Top right:** *An elaborate painted mask found in the kraton of Yogyakarta.* **Middle left:** *The lustre of gold is irreplaceable.* **Middle:** *Mysterious wall relief in Kota Gede, Java.* **Middle right:** *The dashing Kenneth Bensley out and about in Luang Praban, Laos.* **Below left:** *Buddah's image decorated with offerings in a northern Thai temple of Wat Phrathad Lampang Luang.* **Below middle:** *At more than 3 thousands years old, these Egyptian glass eyes still appear quite alive.* **Below right:** *Skilled artisans in Asia have left behind a rich legacy of anonymous art works that continue to provide inspiration for the younger generations This colorful relief is found as a side panel on the peacock gate in the Jaipur City Palace in India.*

EYES THAT INSPIRE

Bensley and Bunnag travel widely and frequently, and these travels are always well chronicled, providing a vast reservoir of images and experiences. As Bensley defines it: " A 'good' day is one where I shoot 9 or 10 rolls of film."

The sense of lively, searching curiosity is evident in these vivacious records, both in the form of prodigious sketches and photographic transparencies. The collected images and fleeting glimpses are as diverse as the countries themselves, and certainly as biased as a personal vantage point has to be. Yet the sense of physical beauty - and in particular, the love for ornamentation, decoration and details - are highly evident. The physicality and sensuality of decoration, especially in traditional structures and crafts, are tributes to sensitive human interaction with nature.

The noted Barcelona architect and theorist Ignasi de Solà-Morales, in his book "Differences", argues that decoration has the potential "even (to) lend itself, in Walter Benjamin's terms, to a reading that is not attentive but distracted, and which thus offers itself to us as something that enhances and embellishes reality, making it more tolerable, without presuming to impose itself, to be central, to claim for itself that deference demanded by totality."

Bensley and Bunnag have long observed and argued that traditional vocabularies of forms offer endless, great lessons for designers. This is perhaps best summed up by critic David Klob, who argues that "traditional vocabularies might be used and metaphorically changed in ways that affirm a solidarity that is not that of shared immediate belief, a solidarity that remains comfortable with future reinterpretation. There is room for buildings that are neither naive celebrations nor elitist games."

Page 16, From left to right, first row: Intricate carved details in a building in Nepal. Colorful and whimsical patterns in the traditional crafts of India continue to inspire many contemporary Asian designers. A brightly colored courtyard wall of an art gallery in Oaxaca, Mexico, inspired Bunnag and Bensley not to be afraid of colour. Second row: Paving details in the plaza of a 17th century church in Oaxaca, Mexico. A lone figure juxtaposed amongst the finely sculpted columns of a traditional structure in the dreamy Durbor Square of Baktapur, Katmandu Valley, Nepal. An intricately carved detail of a stone panel found in a wall at Kota Gede, near Yogyakarta, Indonesia. Third row: Colorful pigments for sale in Katmandu. A humorous fountain detail in Tivoli Garden, Italy. A colored mirror artwork on a temple wall in Luang Praban. The dramatic colors and dazzling play of light are awe-inspiring.
Below: An interesting wall detail, executed in golden sandstone, located in Yucatan, Mexico.

FORMS AND TRADITIONS

"STRONGHOLDS OF TRADITIONS"

"Though human genius in its various inventions with various instruments may answer the same end, it will never find an invention more beautiful or more simple or direct than nature, because in her inventions, nothing is lacking and nothing superfluous."

Leonardo da Vinci

Tropical Asia has an amazingly divergent collection of regions and people, as well as stunning landscapes and natural settings.

There are also rich and textured variations of vernacular architectural styles. The variety seems endless although the term "vernacular architecture" is one of the most commonly used but least understood terms in the region. Vernacular structures, which are in essence "architecture without architects", provide many basic lessons for architects.

These time-proven indigenous shelters were invariably built by anonymous local craftsmen who used local techniques and materials. Such dwellings are well adapted to the extremes of climate and their particular environmental settings. They reflect their own society's accumulated wisdom and collective images. Imbued with cosmological and religious values, social and political structures, their form and decoration are important symbols. They do not have aesthetic pretensions; hence their generating principles are devoid of any straining after originality.

In vernacular settlements, the architectural language is deeply embedded as tradition. Such tradition assures the continuity of vernacular settings through codified imagery, materials and technology. Forms and symbolism are empirically known and stable while change occurs in an incremental manner.

At the same time, architectural forms are not immutable. They have never stay stagnant as a 'pure' culture. They have always been hybrids of indigenous and imported types. These linked series of precedents are part of the creative process of cross-fertilization. They have been diffused, hybridized, and in the process, synergized. Each in turn becomes a potential model that generates further transformations. However, cultural processes and external forces took a long time to reach established states in traditional societies. Once established, these paradigms were sustained for similarly long periods of time.

In Asia, European colonialism in the 19th century resulted in new paradigm shifts that were imposed literally overnight. An unequal socioeconomic and cultural exchange resulted in the emergence of "reinvented" traditions. In the process of stripping away local cultural identities, certain types of hybrid architecture and urban

forms emerged, and which eventually gained acceptance.

Raymond Williams points out that what pass off as "cultural traditions" or "the significant past" are actually selective traditions: " From a whole possible area of past and present, certain meanings and practices are chosen for emphasis, certain other meanings and practices are neglected and excluded . . . Some of these meanings and practices are reinterpreted, diluted, or put into forms which support or at least do not contradict other elements within the effective dominant culture." Hence, traditions are always contested, transformed, resisted and invented.

In Asia, these traditional settings are being rapidly changed and transformed. New projects face the challenge of presenting solutions to the issues of the relationship between tradition and modernity. Architectural theorist Juhani Pallasmaa poses what he sees as one of the essential questions of the architectural profession today: "Can architecture re-create a tradition, a shared ground which provides a basis for the criteria of authenticity and quality?"

One of the six themes he suggests for the re-enchantment of architecture at the turn of the millennium includes "Authenticity", which he defines "more as the quality of deep rootedness in the stratification of culture." He further argues that "as our existential experience looses its coherence through the mosaic of placeless and timeless information, we become detached from traditional sources of identity . . . Authenticity of architectural works supports a confidence in time and human nature; it provides the ground for individual identity."

Page 21, From left to right, first row: The elaborately tiered roofs of a temple in Luan Praban, Laos. Intricate details of a gateway in monochromatic hues. Finely proportioned silhouette of a temple in Nepal. ***Second row:*** *Detail of a curved roof in Jaipur. Multi-tiered roof structure in Nepal. Sandy courtyard of a temple in Luang Praban, Laos.* ***Third row:*** *Sunset view of the Uluwatu temple in Bali. Intricate carved details in a building in Nepal.* ***Below:*** *Nepali figurines on a building's roofline in Patan.*

INSPIRED BY TRADITION

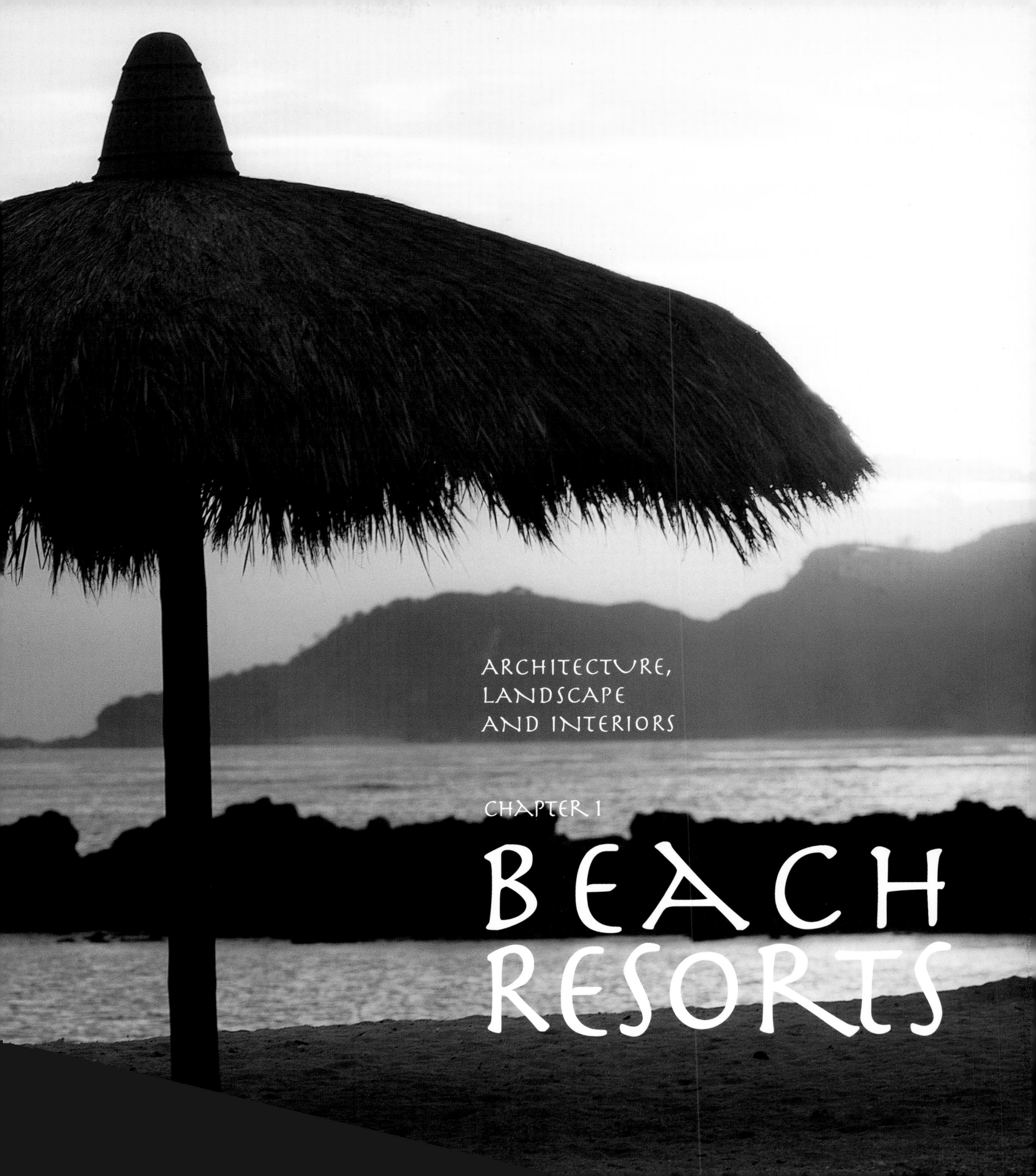

ARCHITECTURE,
LANDSCAPE
AND INTERIORS

CHAPTER 1

BEACH
RESORTS

"HANG LOOSE"
NOVOTEL LOMBOK, INDONESIA

Opposite: *Geckos hewn in stone climb the walls of the pool. Alligators peer around corners while salamanders carry the trellis.* **Top left:** *The bungalow porch floor is finished with polished, salmon-colored render, whilst unhewn wood is used for the columns. The eaves of the "alang alang" roof is left untrimmed to hang loose.* **Top right:** *View of the carved and polished cement columns at the arcade of the meeting rooms.* **Below left:** *The raised rectangular lap pool in front the "Empat Ikan" restaurant overflows on all four sides. From the restaurant, the pool's water level is the same as the dining tables.* **Below right:** *Aloe and yucca are perfectly suited for the hot dry climate.*

Many new five-star resorts and boutique hotels are now designed with an astutely crafted material richness. New players continue to build resorts that are a further affirmation of this particular tendency. Even in the lower-star categories of hotels, a perceivably similar style is emerging.

Architects of such works are producing an architectural ensemble that is well crafted and possesses a sure sense of place. The recently completed Novotel Lombok is an interesting addition to the lower-star category of resort architecture because it shares many of the concepts and ideas found in the already well-accepted pattern of drawing lessons from the local vernacular. At the same time, it differs in the manner in which its architectural proportion and vocabulary are confidently explored.

Located in Putri Nyale, at the remote and beautiful Kuta Beach in Lombok, the Novotel is the first hotel of the Lombok Tourism Development Corporation's planned resort community. This island east of Bali offers stunning natural landscapes, and many new projects in the pipeline may see it challenging Bali as a tourist destination in the future.

Page 27, Top: Rendered drawing of the elevation of the bungalows. Below left: The roof profiles of "Kafe Chili" silhouettes sharply against the sky. Below right: Inside a scaled-down pavilion in the desert garden, there is a beautiful vase made from cementitious ceramics by Philip Lakeman and Graham Oldroyd of Pesamuan Ceramics based in Bali.

Left: The 3-storey block of guest accommodation is carefully articulated to break down its overall scale.

Background: Bunnag's conceptual drawing of the main block.

Top left: *The resort's beach at Putri Nyale is world class.* **Top middle:** *The doors of the meeting rooms are made of carved and laminated coconut wood.* **Top right:** *This carved stone piece is based on of one of the few known "original" early statues found in Lombok.* **Middle left:** *Water pours from the beaks of stone birds at the children pool.* **Middle:** *At the intersection of paths, a tiny village of stone houses sits on top of a pyramid-like base.* **Middle right:** *Stone patterns on the wall of the steps going up to the Health Club. The design is based on traditional Yucatan stone-laying principles.* **Below left:** *The columns of the Empat Ikan restaurant and the meeting rooms arcade are decorated with a deep cement render motif. This technique is especially effective when uplit.* **Below middle:** *Close-up of a detail of the metal door to the mechanical room painted by Bensley's artists in Bali.* **Below right:** *Many of the walls are finished with mud mixed with cement to add strength and applied by hand.* **Opposite:** *The front elevation of the men's comfort pavilion. Light comes down from the wide finial at the roof.*

Designed by Lek Bunnag and Bill Bensley, the 108-room resort is an enticing project that defies easy categorization. Drawn from the indigenous Sasak culture, it is given a playful, improvisational spin. Details are also inspired by the traditional structures from other regions of Indonesia and by places as far away as Mexico.

Turning against the established trend of "Less-is-More" precept, it intensively expresses itself in a highly effusive and celebratory manner. Faced with severe budget constraints, the designers labor hard to make every design move counts. As Bensley describes it: "We wanted the project to be very different in order to make the guests curious, and to make them brave the four-hour journey from Bali. We did not hesitate to move from what we usually do in terms of our design language."

The end result is an invigorating juxtaposition, where the landscape demonstrates flashes of wit and drama, whilst displaying innovation in abundance. Bunnag compares the process to Chinese ink paintings, where "the Master paints the fish, crab, vegetables, grasshoppers…in fact, anything that has to do with the fascinating organic life around him."

Bunnag credits Bensley for the initiation of the "primitive- concept": "Bill came up with the idea of letting loose the edges of the thatch roof to make it different from the way it is being done in Bali, and to achieve

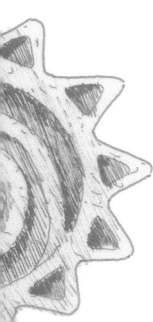

a more primitive look. This started a chain of thought process revolving around the idea of primitiveness."

A variety of different roof forms - from the "upside-down ice cream cones" that cap the Kafe Chili restaurant to roofs with long finials made of alang-alang, a native grass, and ijuk, a black-palm fibre – provides an undulating roof silhouette to what is otherwise a totally flat site. Bunnag also breaks down the scale of the three-storey guestroom block through the deliberate use of a low-hanging thatch roof.

Twenty-three private bungalows, each with its own colorful gardens and exuberant gates, provide important counterpoints to the layout. Throughout the grounds of the resort, tropical vegetation is massed in a mix of dense and self-referential manner, and juxtaposed with drier landscapes and huge doses of sensual sculptural forms.

Page 30-31: *The design of the resort was inspired by the nearby village of Sade.*
Opposite: *The arcade of the meeting rooms overlooks sand paths and river stones which are accentuated by sculptural planting.*
Top: *The concept drawing of the "Empat Ikan" restaurant is playfully sandwiched between two bodies of water - the pool and the sea.*

Opposite: *One of the many conical roofs of the Kafé Chili.*
Top: *This primitive "bus stop" is often used to house traditional Sasak weddings.* **Above:** *Old-fashioned woodcut prints of various areas in the gardens are used as framed decorations in the guest rooms.*

The involvement of the designers was almost total. Bunnag also designed the interiors and the furniture while Bensley conceptualized the restaurants' themes ("Empat Ikan" fine dining restaurant and "Café Chili" restaurant) as well as the design of menus and signage.

The project resonates with unexpected polarities – between complexity and simplicity, abandon and control, privacy and theatricality. Swerving from the reticence and austerity of many recently completed hotels, the Novotel ostensibly veers towards the provision of an architectural backdrop that is supposed to be fun, witty and relaxed.

In the final analysis, the Novotel veers perilously close to an overt display of romanticism. But the architectural control is undeniable, and the scheme has been carefully thought through in all aspects. Proportion and details are handled in a truly tectonic sense, as opposed to paper-thin embellishments and fake materials. Without doubt, the project sets a new precedent, and certainly generates debates on issues related to the reinvigoration of tradition and its place in the discourse of architecture.

Page 36-37: Concept drawing of the massing of "Kafe Chili" Restaurant.
Opposite: *All of the bungalows have a bit of the garden carved out of the resort especially for them. Bensley calls this stone sculpture, "Butthead does Lombok".*
Top: *Interior view of the bungalow - cement render is used on the wall in a polished state up to plinth level and left unpolished to the ceiling level.*

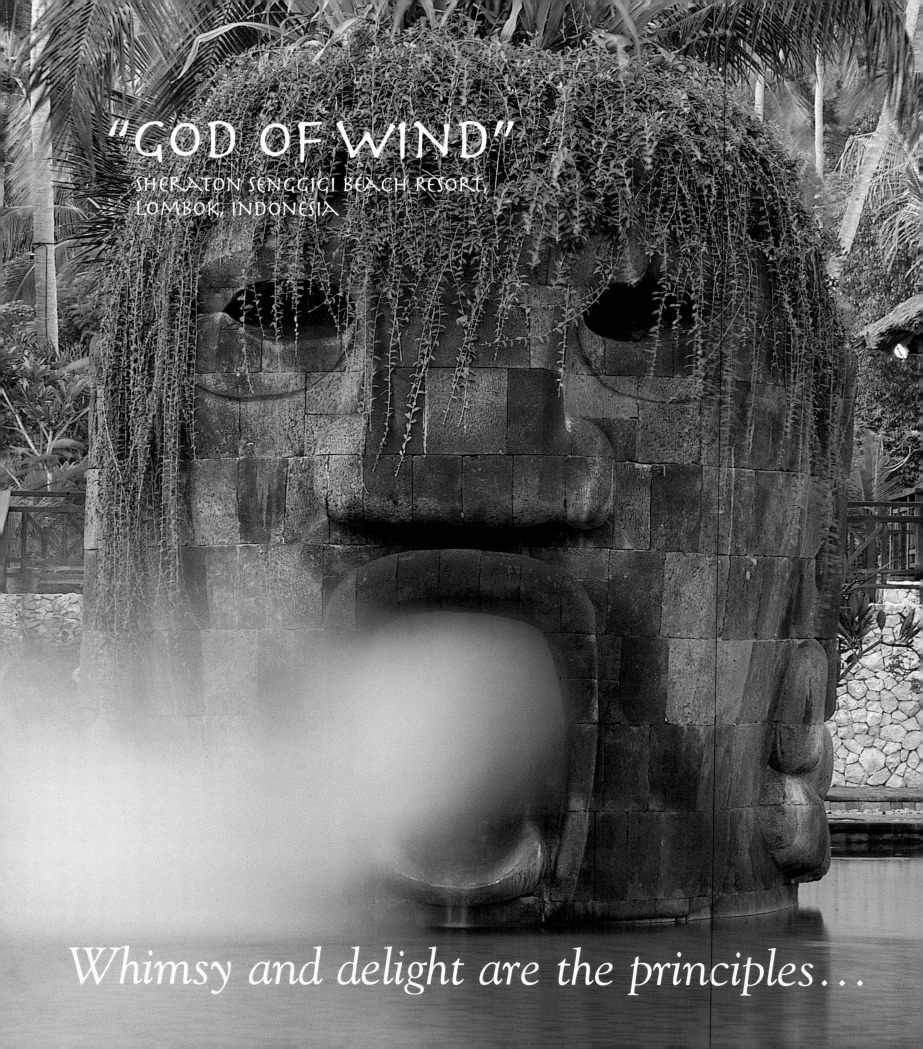

"GOD OF WIND"
SHERATON SENGGIGI BEACH RESORT,
LOMBOK, INDONESIA

Whimsy and delight are the principles…

Opposite: The "Kepala Besar" or Big Head is the focal point of the resort. It was carved from over 300 pieces of andesite stone roughly 500 x 700 x 400 mm in Muntilan, Java. It was numbered, disassembled and trucked to Lombok where it was reassembled and clad to a concrete frame. It measures 7 meters high and 18 meters long. Guests can climb a set of stairs, sit on the back of his giant tongue and slide, through a thick mist, out of his mouth. **Top left:** The hotel comprised of 6 three-storey, single-loaded corridor type buildings. The upper floors have the best sea views while the rooms on the lower floor have large balconies amongst the verdant foliage. **Top right:** The side elevation of the "Kepala Besar" shows his hair and his "ear ring". **Below left:** Traditional dances are held on the stage in the middle of the pool and illuminated by fire. **Below right:** The site originally was a 60-year old coconut grove.

This 165-room resort on a six-hectare coconut grove is also located on the island of Lombok. Designed by Singapore architect Chan Sau Yan and landscaped by Bensley, the chief design feature is the huge swimming pool, an 8,000 square-foot fantasy water feature sets amongst lush gardens. A large torch-lit stage occupies the center of the pool. Its radiant effervescence at night suggests a luxurious and exotic setting.

But the main focus of the pool is an enormous stone head, modeled after the indigenous Sasak's God of Wind. It is a six-meter high, 15-metre long water slide, made of some 300 pieces of black andesite stone. Carved in Central Java, the huge sculpture was transported to Lombok and assembled on site. This Kepala Besar, or "Big Head", stands out boldly in the aquatic environment. For Bensley, this pool is one of his favourites. As he puts it: " It is the first pool I designed under my own practice. It has many of the elements critical in good pool design: edges, stage, fire and drama."

The lush tropical environment is full of surprises and idiosyncratic touches. Whimsy and delight are the principles that guide the design of the entire project. At every turn, unexpected stone objects in the nooks and corners of the grounds and poolside surprise and amuse. Tortoises and crocodiles carved out of black volcanic rocks form part of the poolscape. Other delightful stone carvings are also strategically placed all over the vast grounds.

This is a rich landscape of retreat and renewal, offering both visual calmness and sensory pleasure. The palpability of unadulterated materials, especially in the use of natural stones, is a joy to experience. The resort's grounds surprise guests with palpable qualities of materiality and a real sense of place. The interweaving of building, site and culture offers evidence that an invigorating reinterpretation of traditional lessons can produce a pleasurable yet relevant contemporary landscape.

Left: The lush "Kebun Angrek" or orchid garden, is located between the swimming pool and the main restaurant. **Below:** *The "Kepala Besar" or Big Head has the visual effect of a breathing creature.*

43

Top: *The beach edge of the main swimming pool allows guests to enter the pool gracefully.* **Opposite:** *Masterplan drawing of the pool area. All the elements essential for resort pool design - 50m lap pool, beach edge, sculptural objects and fire elements - are used to create a pool that takes time to explore.* **Opposite below, from left to right:** *A happy stone alligator. The salmon limestone gate to the presidential villa. Inside the "Kepala Besar" is a tongue-like slide. After eight years, the "Kepala Besar" is covered with the vine 'ficus pumila'. Bensley feels that no artificial light can take the place of fire, especially when combined with traditional dance performances. "Fire evokes one's primordial sense," says Bensley. A stone fish with bronze lips provides a refreshing shower. The pool bar seats are whimsically designed.*

Top left: *Both villas have private pools.* **Top right:** *The extensive park-like grounds are immaculately maintained.* **Below:** *This bashful sculpture was carved by famous sculptor Wayan Cemul of Ubud, Bali.* **Opposite:** *This Majapahit-style, soapstone sculpture is decked out daily.*

TANJUNG JARA
TRENGGANU, MALAYSIA

Opposite: *A river divides the property.* **Top left:** *The long sweeping roofs and low eaves provide protection from the monsoon rains.* **Top right:** *The wooden eave detailing typifies the traditional Malay houses.* **Below left:** *The column bases are generously proportioned.* **Below right:** *The pond-side corridor connects meeting rooms to the restaurant.*

Located on the east coast of Malaysia, 65 km south of Kuala Trengganu, this complex was one of the winners in the Aga Khan Awards for Architecture in 1983. Instituted in 1980, the triennial Awards seek to heighten awareness of Islamic culture while emphasizing great value on the social, cultural and environmental aspects of architecture.

The original architects for the project, Wimberley Whisenand Allison Tong and Goo of Hawaii did an excellent job in integrating the architecture with the culture of the picturesque Malaysian east coast. The original hotel consists of 100 guest rooms dispersed in small blocks.

In 1997, Bunnag and Bensley were engaged to renovate the resort in order to make it more competitive in the new millennium. Respecting the original design, Bunnag deftly added a larger lobby, a new library and several meeting rooms, as well as a spa and a restaurant. The design was inspired by some of the best features of Malaysian indigeneous architecture. Overall, this is a textured landscape of tranquillity, offering great visual calmness. The resort's grounds surprise guests with palpable qualities of serenity and tectonic qualities. The interweaving of form, site and culture has been done with great finesse.

Opposite Top: Bunnag feels that the test of a good architect is in the design of "connectors". This one connects the lobby to the restaurant. *Opposite below left:* Slanted perforations provide views of the ocean while providing privacy for the diners on the deck behind. *Opposite below right:* Vegetative motifs are used as decorative elements.
Right: The open-air lobby has a wide overhanging roof.
Below left: Soothing gamelan music can be heard nightly.
Below middle: The staff is mainly recruited from the local town of Trengganu. *Below right:* The river runs under the dining deck.

"TRADITIONS REVISITED"

NOVOTEL BENOA, BALI

This was an exhilarating, fast track project for the architect and the landscape designer because the entire scheme, from the start of design work to the opening day, took less than a year.

Located on the fringe of Nusa Dua, beside the Tanjung Benoa Beach in Bali, the Novotel Benoa offers a Balinese-village atmosphere using the traditional thatch roof as the main architectural vocabulary. The designers Bunnag and Bensley completely renovated a dilapidated, run-down hotel and transformed it into a totally different environment. As Bunnag describes it: "When I first arrived at the existing hotel, it had a large gloomy lobby, and there were only two backpackers in the empty 290-room hotel. I realized the great importance of natural light in interior spaces. Apart from this, there was absolutely no presence of the sea, although the building was only 60 meters away from the beach."

The new-looked resort is now operating so successfully that plans for future extension in the adjacent plot of land have already been drawn up. All the new rooms will have sea views, whilst ground level rooms have private pool corners with cabanas in the water.

Individual guestrooms in standard blocks are compact, but well designed. These 180 rooms are spread over intimate but lushly landscaped gardens. There are also 12 beach cabanas. Each has its own private garden and the now "ubiquitous" open-air bathtub found in the best Balinese resorts.

The resort is divided into two portions by the approach road, with accommodation being split across two parcels of land. A simple porte cochere leads to the reception lobby, which is voluminous and highly dramatic, but detailed with simple means. Architecturally, the details are both Balinese in inspiration and execution. They exploit an already well-established vocabulary of forms.

Page 52, Twelve different cabana designs and a sandy floor make up the beach restaurant "Cocos". Page 53, The biggest problem the designers faced was the difficulty of merging the parts of the resort bisected by a major road. Page 54, Top left: The finely latticed timber screens, held between the columns in the lobby, define a space within a space under the roof. Top right: At the "Crocokiss" Bar, Bensley carved the column bases to resemble reptilian skins. Below left: Water loungers are the focal points of the pool. Below right: Interior view of the main lobby.
This page, below left: A stone sculpture at the pool. Below right: Built over lily ponds, guests can rest on pillows in this unusual pavilion.

An interior view of the dining pavilion or floating bale.

The elaborate roof truss displays a tectonic intricacy found in traditional structures, but executed in much more heroic proportions. Timber columns rest on tapered concrete bases. Huge but finely laced lattice screens add a sense of enclosure to the open structure. Open-sided linkways connect this structure to the restaurant block behind. Bunnag knocked down all walls in the public areas, except for the kitchen and offices. Views are carefully framed whilst movement is deliberately orchestrated to take advantage of the landscape.

Below: The resorts masterplan works despite being disected by a major road.

Page 59, Top left: Each of the beachside bungalows has a private bathing garden. **Top middle:** *The interior of the beachside bungalow is designed with a simple palette of materials and colours.* **Top right:** *A unique feature in the crocodile pool is this overflowing bowl of stone fruits.* **Middle left:** *A "primitive" mirror frame hangs on the mud wall at the "Cocos Beach" comfort room.* **Center:** *The roof forms are cladded in thatch to give a 'primitive' look.* **Middle right:** *The sunken lap pool provides serious swimmers an additional option. It was sunken to create privacy for the guests.* **Bottom left:** *The ordered columns of the lobby.* **Below center:** *Arundo donax versicolor, a grass, almost white, burns bright in the daylight.* **Below right:** *This detail at a Balinese temple inspired the "floating Balé".*

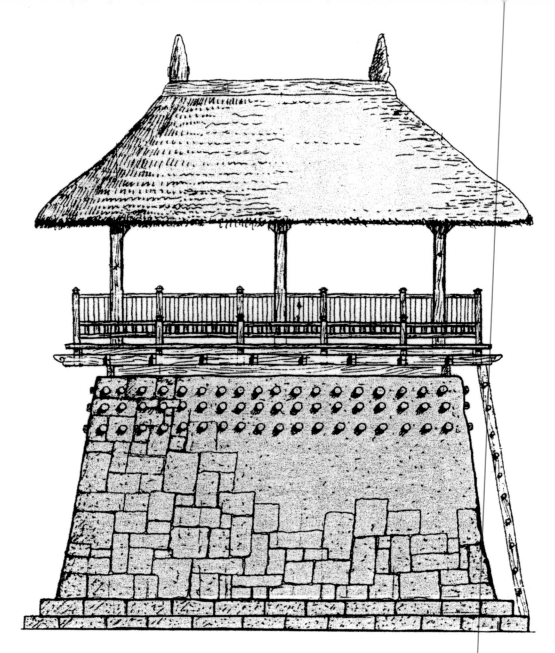

The varied and manifold delights of the gardens and three swimming pools are a pleasure to experience. The beachside pool is renovated by changing all the finishes and floating a series of alang alang-roofed gazebos over the pool's surface. The main stage is surrounded by a series of 12 stone torches and flanked by an elevated music pavilion. A lap pool was created by excavating and lowering the pool below the natural level by some two metres. This allowed the designers to provide a greater sense of privacy for both the pool user and the guests in the rooms.

Careful placement of sculptural artifacts - like enlarged pineapple motifs and female figurines in various poses - enhance the overall effect of the gardens. Bunnag describes the concept as "keeping the architecture under-stated and allow the landscape to express its beauty." These gardens are blended with the architecture as a coherent statement. At the same time, the strong touch of whimsy that pervades the entire rational architectural composition is highly evident. Non-rational forms sharpen the senses and heighten perception. It is a place of continually varied sensations. Yet the execution is confident and commanding.

Above: *Drawing of the musique pavilion. Performers climb this ladder nightly.*
Opposite: *Bunnag wanted clean lines in the lobby to contrast highly with the chaotic streetscape of nearby Nusa Dua village.*

THE GARDENS OF BATUJIMBAR

SANUR, BALI

Opposite: *Just south of Batujimbar in Sanur lies*
known Bali Hyatt. Bensley's first commission in B
was to design the beachside swimming pool. Th
antiquity -"Elephant Cave" - was used as a
inspiration.

This page: *A 6-post bale at the Kajima Residence i*
with white canvas curtains and appears as a
oversized lantern in the vast gardens.

Bensley has been involved in the planning and construction of these properties and ever-evolving gardens since 1985. They include the Wantilan Lama, Kajima Estate, House A and Bali Hyatt. Each of these gardens is a picturesque ideal that has been superbly crafted by the consummate skills of the local gardeners. The sheer effort and conspicuous energy channeled into the project are evident.

The Wantilan Lama gardens are one of the largest in Batujimbar. Bensley designed the naturalistic tropical lagoon pool with a waterfall gated-grotto. Highly animated by an interplay of solidity and transparency, color and light, the house is a product of deft hands and sure eyes. Designed with an organizational simplicity in mind, the artificial separation of inside from outside is broken down. Horizontal movement through the house and its vast grounds is an important design consideration, and perhaps the most compelling aspect of the design.

The two-acre beachside Kajima Estate, built with a relatively high budget, is a designer's dream. Bensley originally designed the landscape for the estate in 1985, and he has been involved with renovations and maintenance to this day.

The gardens were completely rejuvenated in 1995. This exquisite estate, with the building's roofs rising ethereally above the landscape, includes a large open-sided pavilion (wantilan), master's quarters, and eight guest houses, each with its own garden and unique theme. Bensley's favourite is the Nusa Dua garden, a hot and dry collection of native cactus. This is in stark contrast to the rest of the lush grounds.

Bold displays of foliage are carefully framed as part of the views from the interiors. The quality of ever changing light glimpsed through the foliage is especially magical in the early morning. The ambiguous relationship between inside and outside is exploited to provide a thoroughly memorable atmosphere of serenity essential for a holiday dwelling. Pools, walls and landscape coalesce to bring a great sense of serenity and lightness.

Page 65: *A painting by Bensley Design Studios (after Donald Friend's painting of the houses and gardens of Batujimbar).* **Top left:** *The Library Gardens of Wantilan Lama.* **Top middle:** *Every home in Bali must have a small house for the spirits.* **Top right:** *View of the intricate water courtyard at the Kajima Estate.* **Middle left:** *This morning glory is considered a weed.* **Center:** *The beachside dining sala with a bamboo shingle-roof sits on top of an interpretation of Balinese rice fields.* **Middle right:** *In the most private of courtyards, a fish "swallows" one of the columns of a pavilion.* **Below left:** *Dedicated to the owner on his 50th birthday, this statue was erected for one of Indonesia's greatest men.* **Below middle:** *The daughter of the head gardener walks through the white garden.* **Below right:** *The swimming pool is finished with dolowhite plaster dyed beige.*

Top left: *A beautiful white coral gateway filled with bursting blooms of crimson bougainvillea.* **Top middle:** *While croton provides great accent orange color, it also needs constant replanting in semi-shady gardens.* **Top right:** *Coral is no longer allowed to be harvested from the beaches around Bali.* **Middle left:** *View of Wantilan Lama's much-photographed grotto pool.* **Center:** *Bensley's first of many alligator sculptures at the Bali Hyatt.* **Middle right:** *The entrance to the "love grotto". Inside is a tropical waterbed.* **Below left:** *"Rangda", the Balinese mythical witch, and one of the many sculptural objects found in the gardens, is the guardian of the "Lady Garden".* **Below middle:** *Frequented in the past by Mick Jagger, the pool at "House A" was designed by Bensley with a white stone theme in 1989.* **Below right:** *For the Balinese, frogs are a constant source of fun.*

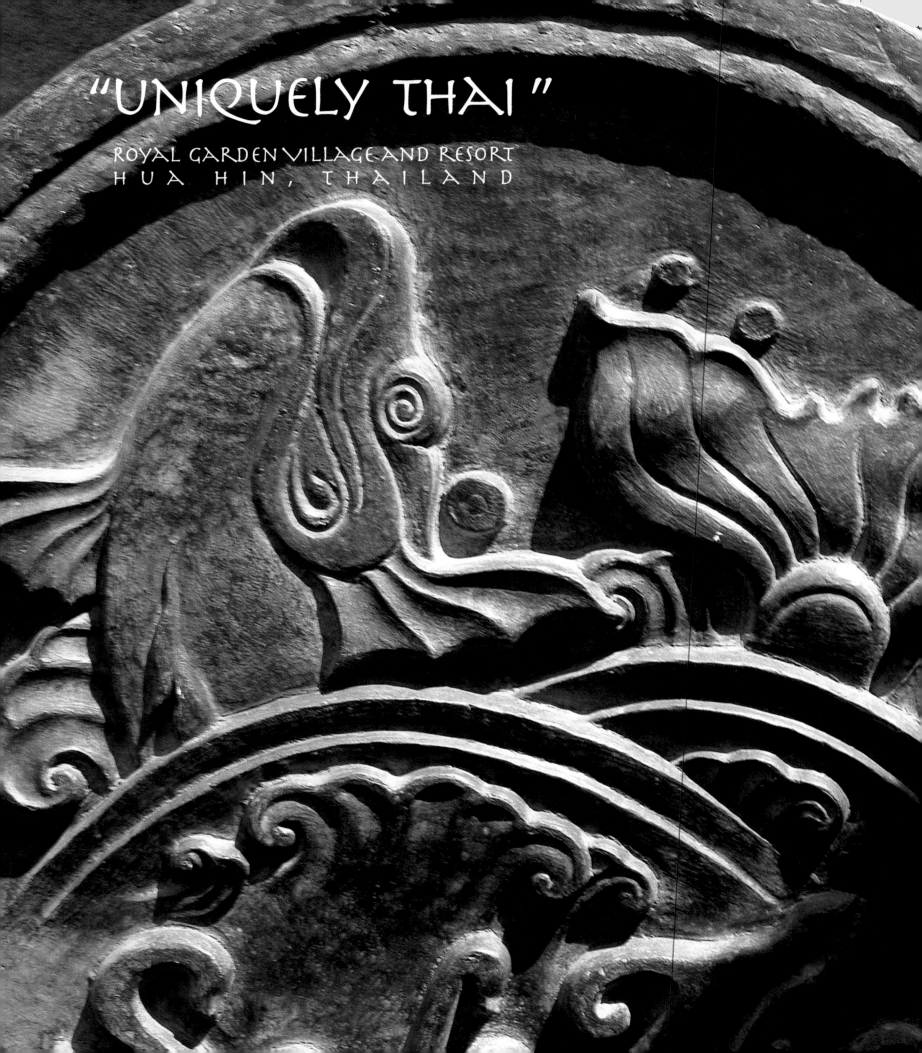

"UNIQUELY THAI"

ROYAL GARDEN VILLAGE AND RESORT
HUA HIN, THAILAND

Designing tropical gardens as a series of vignettes or individual stories, Bensley's approach can best be summed up by his observation that "beauty is created when there is no clear, expected boundary. Tropical architecture should embrace the landscape, and invite it into its deepest rooms."

This is perhaps most succinctly illustrated at both the Royal Garden Village and the Royal Garden Resort in Hua Hin. The two resorts are located about 10 km apart.

Bensley often calls the former his "pet project". His studio has been in charge of the gardens and pools in this intimate beach resort since 1990, about two years after the resort opened. Thai architect Chulathat Kitibutr designed the building complex while Robert G. Boughey was the architect for Royal Garden Resort.

The existing pool in the Village was refinished and new cabanas were added, while new plants were introduced to the grounds. A banana garden was filled with a huge array of musa (banana) and heliconias. There are altogether about 45 different species of musaceae now.

The existing lobby was renovated in 1999. Artists from Bensley's office worked on it for two months, transforming the place into a sensually strong interior. Layers of black and orange paints were added to all the custom-made, oversized furniture, giving it a distinctly "Thai" ambience. Shades of saffron, olive, red and brown dominate. Three-metre wide umbrellas were wrapped with mosquito nets and hung over huge sofa beds. Red antiques, a new series of large paintings in primarily red colors, as well as daily fresh cuttings of hibiscus and red gingers add to the overall rich color scheme.

Infusing rationality with the expressive potency of light and space, the gardens are brought to life at night with a series of coconut oil lanterns placed amongst lush foliage. Plants are used to define space, provide privacy, frame views and create spatial sequences. Spaces overlap and frame vistas. At a peaceful corner next to the sea is a delightful "white" garden, where the plants have either predominantly white foliage or flowers. This is further accentuated by sculpture and pottery painted in white.

This project has matured in a unique way. More importantly, it has been positively transformed by the passage of time.

Page 69: View of the Rim Nam Restaurant at dusk. In this romantic poolside restaurant, great Italian food is served in a Bensley designed interior.

Opposite: Every object in the lobby is either selected and refinished by Bensley's artists or crafted in his studio. ***Below left:*** *The Red Lobby of the Village is specially designed to create an intimate and "uniquely Thai" interior environment.* ***Below right:*** *The palm garden shown here boasts some 50 species of palms.*

Opposite: With dozens of small fire pots lit and reflected across the surface of the pool, the adjacent "Rim Nam" Restaurant enjoys a very romantic setting. **Top left:** Natural pebbles are a pleasant change from the typical white plastic grilles. **Top right:** The Red Court boasts some 25 species of plants with red foliage. **Below left:** This "spiky plants" garden flanks the entrance drive. **Below right:** A small Thai sala, built in Ayuthaya, was reassembled on this island within the Village's extensive grounds.

From left to right, first row: *Hua Hin, and its surrounds, is the world's number one producer of pineapples. Cabanas provide much appreciated shade from the sun, especially for children. Sculptural bowl provides accent details in the garden.* **Second row:** *There are altogether 12 species of bougainvillea at the botanically oriental gardens. There are acres of water and enormous varieties of water plants. Lounge chairs in the water are popular in helping guests to keep cool.* **Third row:** *Atop the shade cabanas around the pool are white sandstone ducks. Thailand is a native habitat for Asian elephants. The landscape is dotted with a collection of jars.*

74

Above: *The poolscape is composed as an inward-looking courtyard with a series of cabanas and dense landscape to provide privacy for bathers.*

"ONE ISLAND, ONE RESORT"
PANGKOR LAUT RESORT, MALAYSIA

Opposite: A very comfortable living room pavilion looks small when compared to the huge trees in this primary forest. **Top:** *Nestled amidst the luxuriant foliage, this guest room enjoys much privacy and sea views.* **Above left:** *Bensley began to bring plant materials from Lumut as early as 1984.* **Above middle:** *Bunnag has created perhaps one of Malaysia's most photographed resort. "Tropical paradise is your own bungalow over the warm waters of the Malaccan Straits".* **Above right:** *New leaves of a Malaysian native forest tree.*

79

From left to right, first row: A passion flower. Sunset over an emerald bay. H.L. Lim's details are natural and appropriate. **Second row:** The roof eave lends a Malay character. Each of the residences has a unique pool. This pool is perched some 40 meters above the emerald waters of Marina Bay. **Third row:** While much of the shore is rocky, there are some very fine pocket beaches. The amenities are residential and rustic. A wooden screen provides a comfortable "back" to the living room pavilion.

From left to right, first row: *Swimming laps in parallel to the ocean is unique. The variation of roof forms typify Bunnag's work. There are two types of coconuts found here. The smaller "Malay dwarf" produces this sweet nut with great colours.* **Second row:** *This pool offers absolute privacy high above the jungle floor., The daybed is a well-lit reading niche. A primitive stone carving made from grey Balinese soapstone.* **Third row:** *The Malay staircase is reinterpreted. The spiky trunk of the Nibong palm. Thai sandstone was imported for all pool copings and steps.*

Located just off the west coast of the Malay Peninsula, the Pangkor Laut Resort is set on a 121-hectare hilly island, amidst an enchanting environment of lush rainforests and vast expanses of white sandy beaches. Designed by Bunnag and Bensley, the project is a wonderful demonstration of the pair's propensity for seeking strong formal solutions.

Highly animated by an interplay of solidity and transparency, especially the way building structures play off the ambiguities of water surfaces, the resort's accommodation is distributed over two bays. One has 53 villas of which 23 are set on stilts over the water. These are linked to one another and to the island by a meandering timber walkway. Another bay has 59 units built over both water and rocky terrains.

The villas over the water are especially light and elegant. Inspired by Thai and Indonesian precedents, details are reinterpreted in new ways. The interiors are designed by H.L. Lim & Associates. A palette of warm silver greys, woody tans and golden ochres mingle with silent creams and charcoals. Used to offset the richness of timber, the finishes and their exquisite materiality give the interiors an intimate feel.

An exclusive separate enclave, called "Marina Bay", was built as a series of nine private houses. Each of these elegant residences consists of separate pavilions linked in an interesting manner. There are separate pavilions for living, dining, sleeping, reading and bathing. These small pavilions, with their small footprints, are sited between the giant trees of the hilly forest.

The honed simplicity of details result in a tactile architecture that thrills the senses and allow for a full set of experiences. In the pursuit of a return to the essentials of architecture based on sensual engagement with natural materials, the result here is highly commendable.

Below: *This bath floats over the warm ocean waters.*
Opposite: *Set in the tree tops, this "Jacuzzi Pavilion" is the ultimate in luxury.*

Top left: *Simple materials like wood and painted plaster are used throughout.* **Top right:** *The traditional Malay staircase is simplified and reinterpreted in this stairway leading to a water suite.* **Below left:** *The guestroom layout was inspired by the nearby fishing villages on Pangkor Island.* **Below right:** *Much of the existing jungle vegetation was retained.*

84

Labels on image: Malay Porch, Foyer, Relaxation Lounge, Semi Outdoor Verandah

Top: *Colored rendering of a section across a villa on stilts.* **Below left:** *Rendered drawing of a water suite.* **Below right:** *The masterplan of Marina Bay illustrates the individually designed residences. Architecture is by Bunnag Architects, interiors by H.L. Lim, and landscape by Bensley.*

"PURE HAWAIIAN"

FOUR SEASONS RESORT,
HUALALAI AT HISTORIC KALUPULAHU, HAWAII

Opposite: A lone beach heliotrope and a "kava" bowl fire torchere are reflected in the resort's main pool. **Top left**: The natural edges of the lava pool sport a beautiful green patina. **Bottom left**: View of the swimming pool. **Right**: Ohia wood, gathered from the local mountains, is used throughout as sculptural railings.

This project was the result of a competition-winning proposal submitted by Bensley. The design team, including architect John Hill, demolished a five-storey unfinished concrete shell (which Bensley describes as "remnants of a 'traditional' hotel that resembled the starship Enterprise"). The resort was then re-designed into one with a more intimate scale and simple forms.

The resort sits on an incredibly beautiful site where black lava flows right down to the blue, sparkling Pacific Ocean. The concept for the gardens is inspired by the original gardens planted by wealthy settlers on the island a century ago. A simple palette with richly textured composition was used. Green leaves and white flowers dominate. Colorful non-Hawaiian exotic flowering plants were avoided.

Bensley brought to Hawaii for the first time some Asian concepts of resort design like outdoor showers and large fire features. Uplights and landscape lighting were not allowed on this site due to the proximity of an observatory.

What is relaxing here is also the perfection of detail achieved by the rhythmic, sculptural forms of the tactile hardscape. Bensley also opted for seven different swimming pools, some of which are lined with indigenous white sands, creating a refreshing contrast to the typical pools found in many Hawaiian resorts. The resort pool is unique in that its cleansing system consists of thousands of tiny red shrimps that keep the water crystal clear. An existing lava layer was also blasted during construction to a depth of seven meters in order to expose a fresh water aqua fore, which is tidal in nature and is absolutely a delight for swimmers.

For the roofs of landscape structures, the forms were fashioned after traditional Hawaiian boathouses. Fountain grass were woven into small tufts to form the roofing materials.

Opposite: The boathouse is made of traditional "ohia" wood whilst fountain grass is used for the roof. The structure casts a comfortable shade on the jacuzzi below. **Top:** *No chlorine or artificial filtration is necessary in this natural swimming lagoon. Thousands of indigenous tiny red shrimps keep the water crystal-clear.* **Below:** *The 18th hole of the resort's golf course.*

CHAPTER 2
HILL RESORTS

"LANNA LINES AND SUMPTUOUS SILHOUETTES"

REGENT RESIDENCES CHIANG MAI, THAILAND

Set amidst the same idyll environment as The Regent, these luxurious properties have an arresting presence. Expressive of an individual sensibility, this is a condominium development that offers privacy combined with the benefits and convenience of the resort's restaurants, room service and selected facilities. There is also a private swimming pool for the exclusive use of owners and guests.

The estate is located on a 20-acre (60 rai) of lush greenery, with the nearby misty hills forming a picturesque backdrop. Surrounded by towering teak trees, it comprises 24 luxury units housed in ten separate villas. These 3 and 4-storey villas are concerted exercises in form making. They are highly articulated and carefully proportioned, in an obvious attempt at breaking down the scale. The units range in size from approximately 330 square metres to 445 square metres. These are offered in three different layouts - Garden Terrace, Mountain View and Penthouse. The Garden units have their own individual plunge pools, while the Penthouses occupy the top two floors of each villa. Spiral staircases lead up to open-sided pavilions at the top.

Architectural proportion and vocabulary are intensively explored in a celebratory manner. Elements are cleverly juggled together; especially the way steeply pitched roofs are juxtaposed. Ornate latticework and rubbled walls give it a quaintly Oriental imagery that is unique. The masonry base gives it the reassuring gravitas of heaviness and age while the spires and roof finials provide the necessary lightness and elegance.

The eclecticism and studied complexity extend to the interiors as well, where wood is used extensively. Richly patterned and extraordinarily wrought details are employed to evoke the plethora of Asian influences. Immaculate craftsmanship, apparent throughout the development, is a constant pleasure. All of the setting's lush beauty can be enjoyed through large openings everywhere. Every unit is fitted with a large, open kitchen and custom-designed terrazzo baths. A fireplace gives the living room a reassuring solidity and warmth.

The Residences is a provocative piece of work in more ways than one. An assured piece of architecture, it has an innate vigor that is perhaps derived from the intense effort put into the design. Bunnag's deft assembly of materials, in particular timber, gives this seemingly insouciant work a light and uplifting touch. The effect is made much more dramatic at night, when the silhouette of the multi-tiered roofs is sharply etched against the sky.

The end result of the bricolaged aesthetic is an arresting piece of architecture. One witnesses the careful blending of various stylistic influences into a stimulating whole. Rather than being a quotational ploy, the project is a result of a liberal dose of Bunnag's personal sensibility.

Page 93, From left to right, first row: Chiang Mai is clearly the center of Thailand's arts and crafts. The gardeners at the Residences. The breakfast nook is perhaps the most handsome aspect of the Residences. Second row: Many elaborately carved wooden figurines are used as art objects throughout the grounds. The multi-faceted architecture is complex. A ceramic elephant sits on the edge of a private dip pool. Third row: The elevations of this building are inspiring. A stone carving peeps out from amongst the foliage. Rendered drawing showing the Residences against the hills.

Opposite: Carefully sited amongst the existing "deng" trees, the Residences fit into the landscape seamlessly.
Below: From the concept stage, the idea was to plan the buildings around the existing trees so as to make the buildings appear more intimate in scale.

"AN EVER EVOLVING GARDEN"

REGENT CHIANG MAI
CHIANG MAI, THAILAND

Lanna, or "Land of a Million Rice Fields", is the name by which the northern part of Thailand and its unique culture have been known for centuries. Founded in 1296 by King Mengrai, the Lanna Kingdom was greatly influenced by neighbouring Burma, China, Laos and Yunnan. Its disntinctive traditions are still apparent in the modern city of Chiang Mai. Located about 700 km north of Bangkok, this second largest city of Thailand is largely noted for both its cultural heritage and cool climate.

Fondly referred to by the Thais as the "Rose of the North", this beautiful city is situated about 310 metres above sea level and has long been a favourite holiday resort for Thais and tourists alike. Over the last couple of years, many holiday homes and resorts have been built in the green valleys outside the city.

The Regent, which opened in April 1995, clearly stands out as one of the most outstanding projects in this fertile intermontane basin. Located in the sub-municipality of Mae Rim District, the city's first five-star resort is 13 km from the city of Chiang Mai.

This project clearly demonstrates an earnest concern and a keen sensitivity to the pristine environment. The impact of the tropical idyll is immediate and pervasive. Landscaped by Bensley and master-planned and designed by Bunnag, the project was executed by Chiang Mai architect Chulathat Kitibutr of Chiangmai Architects Collaborative. Formulated on a solid underpinning of architectural knowledge, the resort essentially comprises 16 double-storey clusters of four rooms with attached salas or outdoor pavilions.

The prominent, intricately carved crossed bargeboards or kaelae and private gazebos called salas formed part of the design of each of the well-crafted guest pavilion. Overlooking the dramatic Doi Suthep mountains, these raised teak pavilions are integrated with eight hectares of rice terraces and lush landscaped gardens. The bold and innovative use of the rice fields as part of the landscaping strategy is not only unique, but it also brings the resort back to the region's agricultural roots. The rice harvested by the resort's farmers is distributed to charity and hill villages.

The landscape design is probably the most important and memorable element in the resort. Tropical vegetation is celebrated in a manner that can perhaps be best described as one of unbridled enthusiasm and controlled planting, and a sense of the natural juxtaposed with a deliberate sense of artificiality. Linked by numerous pathways made of sandstone and laterite, the various amenities of the resort are sensitively hidden by thick foliage.

This lush tropical environment is full of little surprises. The varied and manifold delights of the gardens are a pleasure to experience. Careful placement of sculptural objects and terracotta reproductions of Khmer art works in the nooks and corners of the grounds greatly enhance the overall ambience.

Another highlight of the gardens is the dramatic experiential difference between day and night. Here is one of the best examples of garden lighting – where the contrast of diurnal moods is so strong. At night, there are hundreds of lights in the property although few are visible during the day. More than 300 small kerosene lanterns, supported on bamboo stands, are lit over the rice fields at night, suffusing the entire place with an almost surreal and totally atmospheric glow.

One of the reasons behind the success of the gardens is that the landscape architect continues to provide consultancy services in order to supervise the gradual evolution of the landscape over the years. As Bensley puts it: "As a garden is never finished, we have a lifetime job!" A sum of about 30,000 baht per month is set aside for the purchase of landscape materials to augment the gardens. Of course, a whole team of 45 gardeners as well as Bensley's partner, Jirachai Rengthong, work hard to keep the gardens in its lush state.

*Page 97: Each of the hotel suites has a private connected dining pavilion. **Opposite top left:** View towards the verdant backdrop of hillscape. **Right:** Laterite pathways gently saunter across the gardens. **Above:** Bunnag's original drawing for the concept of the hotel rooms.*

Top left: *Set dramatically against the hills, this pool overlooks the grounds.* **Top right:** *The gardener tidies a type of grass that is used to make traditional brooms.* **Below left:** *A sculpted wooden figurine of a chubby Thai prince, enjoying a leafy corner of the garden.* **Below right:** *Pathways are set amongst dense foliage.*

Top left: *View of the pool pavilion and spa pavilion.* **Top right:** *The "gaelae" adorns the roof peak of most northern Thai houses.* **Below left:** *Using traditional building methods and brick plaster, these elephants strongly define all four corners of the arrival court.* **Below right:** *This rice barn houses a collection of Thai instruments which the gardeners play for a few minutes everyday at precisely 4:55 p.m. before they return home.*

"LANNA LEISURE"

THE LANNA SPA
CHIANG MAI, THAILAND

Located within the grounds of The Regent Residences, the Spa opened in the beginning of 2000.

Designed by Lek Bunnag, the project features an interesting interpretation of the Lanna Thai culture. Set within a lush landscaped environment, the concept explores the rich heritage of Lanna Thai, as well as notions of privacy and luxury.

Top left: *An oversized bath sits next to generous panels of glazing.* **Top right:** *A verdant leaf overlaps a decorative wooden lintel.* **Below left:** *Elaborately carved details are specially made for the walls of rooms.* **Below right:** *The warm lights accentuate the strong colors in the interiors.*

Top left: *A huge daybed is placed next to a pool of water.* **Top right:** *View of the roof structure seen from the terraces.* **Below left:** *Detail of the gate's roof.* **Below right:** *The sparse simplicity of the interiors provide a calm enviroment.*

Chiang Mai has always been the center of the Lanna Kingdom (established more than 700 years ago). In this project, Bunnag consciously evoked the cultural heritage of this rich kingdom through the planning, execution and detailing of every element. At the same time, there is a conscious attempt to inject a sense of the contemporary through stylized and abstract notions of space and details.

There are a total of 6 Treatment Suites, a Penthouse Presidential Treatment Suite and a Beauty Salon. Four of the Treatment Suites offer private access through garden gates, where guests can be checked-in without passing through the Spa's reception, which is located on the second storey. These Suites have private gardens with their own dip pools.

The unique interiors, inspired by Lanna Thai architecture, are beautifully finished with traditional timber floors and filled with painting, sculptures and traditional patterns of gold-leaf on wood.

Each room is clearly defined by thick masonry walls. At the same time, they are given visual depth through layered views. Bunnag greatly acknowledges the inspiration from existing temples in northern Thailand like Wat Phumin in Nan.

These rooms are also filled with artworks inspired by Lanna Style frescoes, which depicted the everyday life of the people in exquisite poses. Bunnag and his team of artists again reinterpreted these artworks into new paintings, albeit in a more expressive manner. One of the most impressive art works in the Spa is a series of six oversized plastered, painted bas reliefs of the Lanna pattern called "Khanuk". Placed in the reception lounge, these tantalizingly curved forms are further enhanced with thick rice paper finish in order to create a more textured surface.

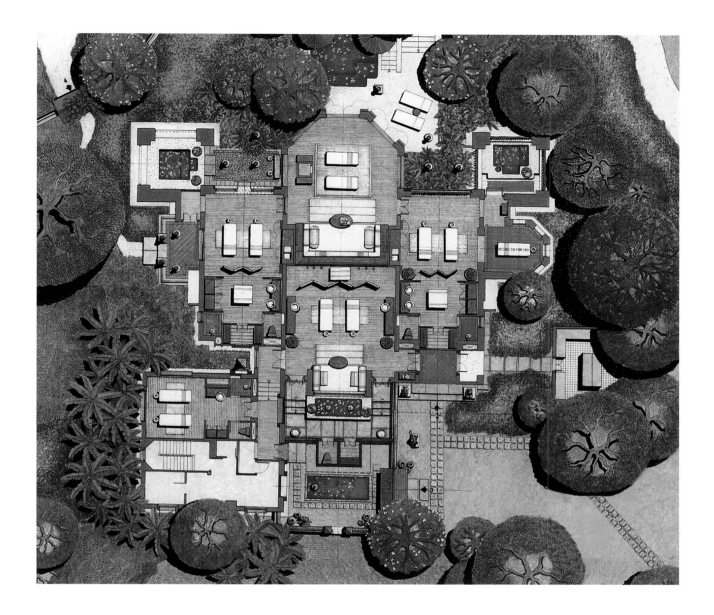

Another distinctive feature of the Spa is the ubiquitous use of gold and maroon colors. These colors, widely used in Lanna culture, are juxtaposed to create interesting effects in dimly lit rooms.

This is a highly polished piece of work, where the use of traditional elements is deployed at a greater level of abstraction. The result is a delightful mix of traditional sensuality and modern sleekness. It is not a design that revels unnecessarily in ornamentation, rather its consistent palette of rich colors and materials ensure its sophistication, and ultimately, luxury.

The late Egyptian architect Hassan Fathy once argued that "when the full power of the human imagination is backed by the weight of a living tradition, the resulting work of art is much greater than any that an artist can achieve when he has no tradition in which to work or when he willfully abandons his traditions." In this age of massive technological achievements, the Spa demonstrates that vernacular traditions are still seen as having a reference point.

In most instances, adopting traditional motifs and using them in such a hybridized manner will definitely provoke howls of protest. Architect Perez-Gomez has observed that "architects often work under the absurd assumption that meaning and symbol are merely products of the mind, that they can be manufactured a priori."

Yet the masterful execution of various 'styles' into an intriguing and convincing whole here is unmistakable. The project's spirit of intuitive invention is wonderfully evident. A fond ode to the enigmatic landscape, this Spa certainly has a compelling vitality wholly its own.

Opposite: *The essence of this project is about diminishing perspectives. With the massage beds in the foreground, the Thai herbal steam room is located beyond the wooden door.*
Top: *Bunnag Architects' rendered floor plan of the Spa.*

"CONTEMPORARY VERNACULAR"

NOVOTEL BOGOR
BOGOR, INDONESIA

This Novotel resort, adjacent to the Novotel Golf Course, is built just outside the city of Bogor in Java, Indonesia. Blessed with excellent soil conditions, the extensive gardens matured very quickly soon after construction.

Coffee Shop   to Reception Court

Tucked sensitively into an existing durian grove, the main swimming pool features three series of copper-lined wooden troughs that drain water from the poolside structures into the pool. A series of bridges was also designed as crossings over a natural stream bisecting the garden.

Bunnag has designed a beautifully crafted, simple, double-loaded, 165 metre-long hotel block. The preference for elemental architectural expression is evident. Although the building is long, a complete image is never fully revealed, but glimpsed in fragmentary ways. The steeply pitched roof is a dexterous elaboration on a simple geometric element, creating a complex series of images viewed from amongst the foliage. Bunnag credits this to influences from his Thai background: " I learnt this technique from the design of temples in Thailand. We add in order to make forms appear more intimate."

The elongated 5-storey block also engages on a highly visceral level, forming a coherent entity within the lush garden setting. It steps down to two stories at the end of the block. Architecture and landscape are fluidly integrated in a rich, unified whole.

"My satisfaction is that this 290-room hotel appears like a single 2-storey house among trees when viewed from the golf course. This helps to preserve the natural look to the adjacent golf course across the stream," says Bunnag.

The building is akin to a choreographer's concern for the delight of movement and discovery. From the reception lobby, the movement is downwards through a series of staircases and enclosed courtyards. Views are carefully framed by a series of openings and perforations in the thick walls, while spaces are richly layered. The allusive vocabulary of forms, manifested through beguiling simplicity, provides further evidence of Bunnag's intuitive touch.

The project clearly demonstrates the vitality of vernacular precedents and spaces, as well as the richness of texture and materials. Monochromatic interior finishes also utilize local materials to great effects, evoking a highly languorous and tranquil feel.

Faced with increasingly demanding guests, hotel developers are forced to look beyond the mere provision of room and recreational facilities. They realize that architecture can make the big difference. In this project, an earnest attempt is made to create architectural forms that recall traditional Javanese structures, and at the same time, incorporates contemporary vocabulary. As architect Christopher Alexander once noted, "There is no perfect static language, which once defined will stay defined forever. No language is ever finished." The architecture of the resort, through its earnest attempt, certainly points towards a possible direction.

Page 108, Below: *Concept drawing of the main block showing a variety of roof forms designed to break down the scale of the mass.* **Top:** *The superb soil and rainy climate of Bogor make for a very lush green garden and privacy for the outdoor bathtubs on the ground floor.* **Below left:** *Bensley designed this playful, turtle-like roofed bridge to cross an existing stream.* **Below right:** *Streams of running water fall over the underwater seats at the pool bar.*
Page 110, Top left: *This pool was primarily designed in the field in order to preserve the mature grove of durian trees.* **Top right:** *This 25-meter lap pool accommodates serious swimmers.* **Below left:** *Bunnag designed the architectural interiors as well as the furniture in this "three-meals" restaurant.* **Below right:** *Three rivulets of water and a "Salacca magnifica" are framed by the end wall of the pool arcade.* **Bottom:** *The masterplan of the resort showing the stream, golf course, and the existing woodlands on both sides.*

THE JAIPUR BLUES

RAJVILAS JAIPUR, INDIA

Built to resemble the ancient palaces on the barren hills of Rajasthan, on the western desert landscape of India, this hotel by the Oberoi Group is an impressive collage of fortified architecture designed by Bombay-based P.G. Patkti, with interiors by the Singapore design firm of H. L. Lim & Associates.

Mr. P.R.S. "Biki" Oberoi,

vice-chairman and managing director of the Oberoi Group, acquired a twenty-six-acre property about five miles east of Jaipur in 1991. This was later expanded to thirty-two acres. After three years, and with more than eight hundred workers crafting the complex, the fort-like resort was completed in sumptuous style.

Bensley was engaged to design the extensive gardens of perhaps India's first real boutique hotel. Set within a former working farm and orchard, the sublime landscape of formal gardens is inspired by traditional Mogul gardens.

Lush manicured lawns are interspersed with beautiful moats, fountains and lotus ponds. Movement through the resort follows a carefully choreographed sequence of overlapping outdoor and indoor spaces through a series of "follies" and view pavilions. The grounds are crisscrossed by elaborate networks of sandstone paths. Handmade Jaipur tiles, in deep shades of blue, stand out prominently under the strong light. For Bensley, the biggest challenge was learning a new architectural language for the design of the hardscape.

The centerpiece of the vast property is a two-hundred-and-fifty-year old Shiva temple, which is located on a small island surrounded by a lotus pond. To its west, a courtyard mansion has been converted into a health club flanked by a traditional herb garden and an extensive lotus pond.

Page112: *Drawing by Bensley Design Studios exhibits the Mogul style of false perspectives. It illustrates the entertainment courtyard, the main lily pond and the guestrooms beyond.*

Page113: *View from a musique pavilion across the formal water courtyard to another musique pavilion.*

Opposite: *Lit primarily by fire, the entertainment courtyard is softened by gorgeous embroidered canvas canopies and lacy sandstone-colored jalis.*

Top: *White marble elephants flank the entrance courtyard. Two musique pavilions break the scale of the main fort.*

The spa building is a lovingly constructed, and faithful renovation of a traditional Rajasthani haveli or farmhouse. The guestrooms are clustered in small groups around courtyards. Architecturally, the complex is influenced by history and crafted with a liberal juxtaposition of various cultures and styles, ranging from Mogul, Hindu to Anglo-Indian elements. Made of local stone and finished with a traditional liming technique, the effusive lyricism of the structures are further imbued with elaborate decorative trimmings.

Individual rooms are equally eclectic, sumptuously furnished with a mixture of loose and built-in furniture that exudes an air of traditional elegance and lightness. Four-posters, tactile cotton dhurrie rugs, solid teak pieces and huge wicker baskets are juxtaposed in a highly effective and personal manner. A scalloped arch sculpted out of the external walls provides a niche for window seating.

This seventy-two-room resort also features 12 guest tents set within informal gardens. The roof membrane, modeled after hunting structures once used by Rajput royalty, provides a graceful enclosure, reminiscent of nomadic tent construction.

Top: Influenced by traditional Mogul herb gardens, this traditional stepped garden showcases, in sharp contrasts, two different types of "alternanthera". **Opposite top left:** A detail of the fine plasterwork at one of the "floating" temples. **Opposite top right:** View from across the entrance courtyard. The solid white marble elephant in the foreground is dressed with fresh flowers from the garden everyday. **Opposite below:** A 250-year old temple sits in the center of the property. It is surrounded by an enormous lily pond, where four "floating" temples are located.

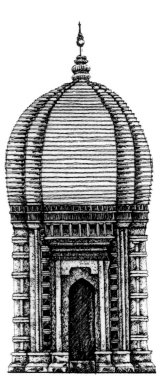

From left to right, first row: *The blue shades of Convolvulus mauritianus. A poolside pavilion is set in the garden of the opulent presidential suite. A smart driver at attention at the front door of the lobby.* **Second row:** *A Jaiselmer stone medalion in the presidential deck depicts the parrots that fly freely in the gardens. This dining pavilion was added at the very last minute during the construction process to open the entertainment courtyard out to the gardens. The craftsmanship in laying the pink Jaipur sandstone, white Italian marble, and black granite is impeccable.* **Third row:** *The water pavilion greets arriving guests. The layering of shady landscape elements provides a moderating factor to the hostile climate. Bensley planted the blue flowering Jacquemontia pentantha. The main swimming pool is lined with locally-made Jaipur blue tiles.*

From left to right, first row : Bensley designed the four new temples placed in the corners of the lily pond. A simple light niche in a thick mud wall is decorated with traditional Rajastani motifs. An antique brass urn in the middle of an eight-sided pavilion. **Second row:** The entrance to every guestroom courtyard is a small pavilion The polished brass star and pot floats just above the surface of the crystal-clear pool water. Sunrise over the swimming pool. The 250-year old temple and the guestroom courtyards are in the background. **Third row:** The border between the pathway and the planter is elegantly terminated by the sandstone carved endcap. A waiter posing casually at the dining pavilion. At the entrance, Indian elements are combined to create an air of fantasies.

CHAPTER 3
URBAN RESORTS

"MADE IN MYANMAR"

KANDAWGYI PALACE HOTEL
YANGON, MYANMAR

One of the most conspicuous symbols of modernity in many parts of the Asia is the "international standard" hotel . This is especially so in the rapidly developing countries of Indochina. Myanmar, in particular, is experiencing steady growth in the tourist trade.

Being the largest country in Southeast Asia, and blessed with a large diversity of natural scenery and superb architecture, Myanmar is one of the most beautiful countries in the region. However, many hotels are still designed in the same Neo-Classical kitsch that has been a blight to all Asian cities. Ill-proportioned and adorned with paper-thin ornamentation, these buildings have an inevitable tendency to homogeneity behind the dressed-up fronts. Besotted with nostalgia and often couched in the plaintive term of "tradition", many offer a superficial reassurance of well-crafted buildings. While some may offer a physicality that is interesting, there is little creative reinterpretation of regional history.

One of the rare few that demonstrates an attempt at creative reinterpretation of the country's rich architectural heritage is the Kandawgyi Palace Hotel in the capital city of Yangon. The exactingly executed hotel, designed by Bunnag and landscaped by Bensley, offers a formal solution that consists of elaborate juxtapositions of various stylistic influences.

The client Bijoux Holdings' brief was a 5-storey tall building. The architectural resolution aims at visually balancing a strong horizontal expression with elegant multi-tiered roofs. Based on surviving traditional skills, the building invariably necessitates the involvement of craftsmen at an early stage. The result is a well-crafted resort that despite its 200-room size, is a tribute to fine artistry.

Viewed from the opposite shores of a serene lake, the building cuts an interesting silhouette.

Though imposing, the building sits very well on the site. The rhythm of the multi-tiered roofs offsets the rigidity of the guestroom elevation. The use of timber shingles for the roof also provides a sense of rusticity to the overall massing.

The entire entrance porch is built in golden teak using Burmese traditional wood constructional method. Its high-volume space immediately sets a tone of controlled grandeur. Closely placed columns in the reception lobby accentuate the sense of vertiginous space.

At the same time, it is tangibly evident that Burmese architectural vocabulary has been intensively explored in a highly engaging manner. Forms are drawn from the traditional architecture of Indochina and juxtaposed, composed and reinterpreted in a highly refreshing manner. Scale is handled in a sensitive way, such that the building retains an intimate feel.

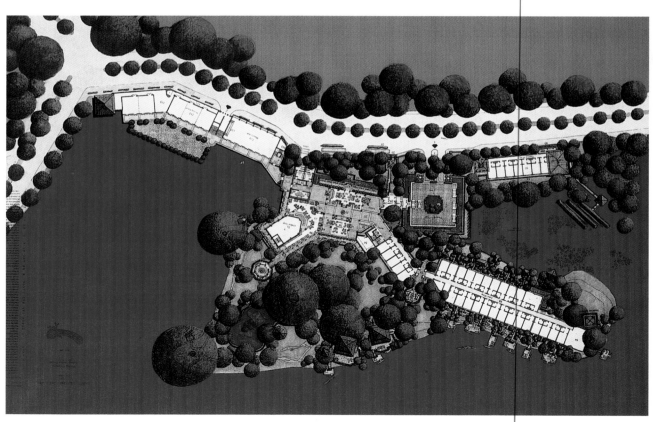

Top left: The "elephant pool" has three different levels that step down to the lake. **Top right:** View across the "banyan tree garden" to the elephant pool and pool bar. **Below left:** This wooden peacock is made from 1 piece of golden teak and stands almost 2 meters high. **Below right:** A walkway outside the presidential suite, decorated with traditional Burmese water containers.

Top left: *A 4-tiered entrance pavilion straddles the pathway to the main guestroom block. It reduces the scale of the building to a more intimate one.* **Top right:** *Ceiling details of the Royal Bungalow.* **Below left:** *The roofs of the lakeside pavilion are crowned with wooden finials which double as lightning conductors.* **Below right:** *A small teak pavilion sits on a painted plaster base. It houses a light that accents a bowl of floating flowers at night.*

127

Immaculate craftsmanship, apparent throughout the development, is a constant pleasure. Ornate eave carvings, richly patterned gable screens and other decorative motifs are handcrafted by local artisans and integrated into the design. The ancient Burmese plaster-painted flower wall element, for example, is used to envelop the entrance car court. Its sheer whiteness sets up an interesting juxtaposition with the darkly stained timber structures.

By setting back the building from the main road, the hotel also achieves a greater sense of presence. Existing mature trees in the property are preserved, hence blending the hotel into the site. The end result is a handsomely detailed resort of great confidence and competence, where site, form and materials have been integrated into an indissoluble whole. Created with an exemplary understanding of site and climate, the layout sets up a rhythm where the guest is in constant contact with the wonderful panorama of nature.

The eclecticism and studied complexity are surely issues of contention among critics and architects, who may question the bricolaged aesthetic of the project. Again, this project's tectonic rigor is undeniable. The building's innate vigor is obvious. One cannot deny the masterful execution of various 'styles' into a compelling personal statement. It has an overall intriguing vitality that is rarely seen in resorts.

In the final analysis, this deftly articulated building has been pulled off with panache. The Kandawgyi Palace Hotel, in making an enlivening contribution to the resort scene, also succinctly raises several pertinent questions relating to issues of quotation and invention.

Page 123: *The focal point as one drives up the entrance route to the porte cochere is the connecting bridge from the lobby to the main block. A Burmese folly crowns the top of the bridge and allows visual transparency across the block.*

Page 124: *Bunnag's original drawing of the west end of the building, illustrating the tiered roofs that help to break down the scale of the structure.*

Page 125, Top: *Great care was taken to build this magnificent teak porte cochere under the canopy of a huge rain tree.*
Below: *The porte cochere has 22 eight-meter long columns specially picked from logs that were brought down the Irrawaddy River.*
Opposite: *The main guestroom wing is reflected in the black pond at the porte cochere.*

"IN THE SUKHUMVIT SKIES"

SHERATON GRANDE SUKHUMVIT BANGKOK, THAILAND

Located in one of the busiest hearts of Bangkok, this new hotel in Sukhumvit Road is certainly one of the best hotels in town. It has a Thai style rooftop pool garden, with panoramic views of Lake Rachada and the Lumpini Park.

The garden is sensitively planned to make the space appears much larger. Eschewing the monochromatic tones of most contemporary hotels, Bensley confidently play with a vibrant color palette. A rich color scheme of charcoals, terracottas and cobalt blues has been employed with great effects. These colors, combined with custom-designed sculpture representing different parts of Asia, make for a new look in the very competitive Bangkok hotel scene.

One of the design intentions was to create a strongly "Thai" garden, but juxtaposing it with sculpture and objects from all parts of Asia. Changes in levels also create an interesting undulating ground plane. Set amid a lushly landscaped and intimate garden, the pool is a tranquil world where the ambience of serenity is totally pervasive.

Page 130: *As seen from the roof top of the hotel, this poolscape is clearly on oasis in frenetic Bangkok.*
Page 131: *This four-faced Thai "sala" pavilion houses a hot Jacuzzi pool. Mirrors are suspended between columns to*

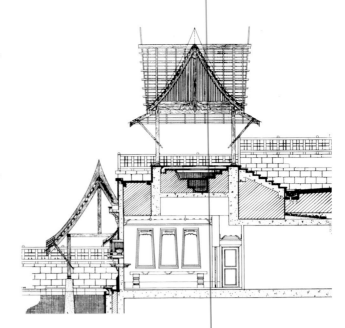

reflect the garden and to block out views of the skyscrapers beyond. **Top:** *Bensley's drawing of the shade sala over the pool, the comfort rooms (in terracotta red) and the private spa for the Garden Suite.* **Middle:** *A long elevation of the grand suite showing the dining sala, sun decks and the cold dip sala.* **Below:** *Rendered drawing of the masterplan.*

Top left: *Three sandstone vessels are carved in the Baan Chiang style.* **Top right:** *Views are cleverly blocked out by plants and accentuated by water features.* **Below left:** *Many of the sculptures have to be "discovered" as the plant growth here is very vibrant.* **Below right:** *This deep-relief terracotta panel is made from Baan Phor Liang Muer in Chiang Mai.*

133

"ETHNIC WIT"
FOUR SEASONS RESIDENCES
JAKARTA, INDONESIA

Opposite: Lit by 4-meter high fire torcheres, this 6-post "alang alang" shade pavilion stands over a bubbly spa corner in the lower swimming pool. **Above, from left to right, first row:** A bridge spanning across lotus and lily ponds is designed to look like an amorphous, organic form. This giant aloe grows to 5 meters tall. Black and tan are the colors that tie the varied materials together. **Second row:** An elaborately patterned wall in the garden. The stone craftsmen of Central Java are adept at both the refined and the primitive. This is the "nasty frog club", with figurines of frogs sticking out their tongues. **Third row:** One of the themes in the landscape is the use of humorous sculpture to portray the various poses of Indonesians from all walks of life. This is a 12 x 4 m high deep-relief sandstone carving depicting the various ethnic groups performing in the same orchestra. A garden lantern sets against a stone wall.

The project took seven years,
and continued through the economic crisis and political
turmoil that radically re-shaped the country. During that
time, Bensley produced over 600 details. It is probably the
only large project that proceeded during that period.
Located in the traffic-choked environment of Jakarta,
this development consists of four towers - all residences -
designed by RTKL Architects. Bensley was commissioned
to design the gardens and pools.

Conceptually, plants are selected for their unusual
foliage, like giant aloe and wodytia. "More is More" also
appears to be the design precept, as an elaborate juxtaposition of heavily textured materials and plants combined
to create a vibrant urban oasis. Bamboo, shingles and
alang alang are used for the roofs of pavilions, while
brown stones from Lombok are set against polished peach
pebbles. There are altogether 24 pavilions or gates, all
designed differently. Three pools provide the main water

features. Six towers, each four metres high, are placed in
the middle of the main pool as "rain showers".

A highly elaborate "batik-like" panel, made of
ceramics and created by artisan Pesamuan from Bali,
stands out in stark contrast through its black tones.
However, the ground's effusive lyricism stands out most
prominently amidst the sleek, modern towers around it.

*Page 138, **Top left:** Inspired by the Lion Court at Alhambra
in Spain, this courtyard is full of whimsical and irreverent lion
figurines. **Top right:** The silhouette of a Javanese woman figure is etched against a stone wall. **Below left:** Another graceful woman figure sits amidst dense foliage. **Below right:** The
chess pavilion rests on retaining walls built out of roughly walls
built out of roughly hewn "Batu Klaten" stones.*

From left to right, first row: *Detail of the pool edge. "Primitive" stone figures dot the gardens. Bensley mixes a wide variety of textures and materials in new ways.* **Second row:** *Textured stone walls provide a sense of great tactility. Flowers like the Anthurium are composed in large-masses. Details of the floor finishes at the corridors.* **Third row:** *Colored pebbles form patterns on the ground. Planters are designed in a variety of forms. The comfort rooms' wall is clad with yellow and blue tiles from Pesamuan, Bali.*

140

From left to right, first row: *At the four corners of the lily pond-bridge stands these 2.5 meters high Indonesian totems. Even the guard houses are cladded with gorgeous textiles. True to the black and tan color concept, umbul umbul or Balinese style flags flank the entrance.* **Second row:** *Each of the four towers has an impressive entrance with cast bronze baskets measuring 3 meters across. Again, cast in bronze, these three-oversized showerheads constantly pour water into the pool. Carved from plantation teak, these hanging lion bowls double as lanterns.* **Third row:** *Pink pineapple is planted extensively at the entrance because its color and texture reinforce the overall design theme. Deep relief ceramics from Pesamuan, Bali. One-meter diameter sandstone stepping-stones are spotted across a field of mondo grass.*

141

"A CALM OASIS IN CHAOTIC BANGKOK"

BAAN BENSLEY
BANGKOK, THAILAND

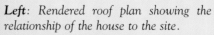

Left: *Rendered roof plan showing the relationship of the house to the site.*
Above, right: *The breakfast area, located at the upper level deck, is shaded by leafy foliage.*
Opposite: *View of the guestroom from the deck at night.*

This Thai pavilion is situated in the suburban district of Soi Chang Ket, off Sukhumvit Road. Traditional timber houses in Bangkok have virtually being wiped out of existence and replaced by largely bland and ill-conceived steel-and glass towers. Hence it is a delight to find this structure in such a context.

The picturesque high gable ends of the roofs are closed off by the distinctive design of the barge board, the most poignant symbol of Thai architecture. The clarity of the construction celebrates the process of its assembly, where every joint and detail is clearly articulated as an aesthetic element.

The entrance courtyard is densely planted, and created a sense of great enclosure. This allows the structure to slowly open up as one moves around it. A simple timber stairs leads up to two traditional Thai pavilions originally from Ayutthaya. Perfectly proportioned, they were reassembled to form two richly evocative garden courtyards.

Remodeled to suit contemporary living, these two pavilions are linked by an open-air timber deck at the second level. Serving as the main living space, this deck is probably the most important and delightful part of the house. It truly demonstrates that although the primary function of a house is shelter, its richness is derived from the simultaneous experience of the interior and the exterior.

On the second level, each pavilion accommodates one small but comfortable bedroom with an attached bathroom. A dining room is located beneath one of the pavilions, while the space beneath the other pavilion houses a kitchen and the maids' quarters.

The warm tones of timber in the interior is complemented by the rich textures of furniture and art objects. Collected from many parts of Asia, these objects offer a delightful tapestry of moods, textures and colors.

Opposite top left: View of the bedroom, where a traditional-style painting drawn in the studio is set into an antique wooden frame. *Opposite top right*: A collection of 19th century Indian "jalis" and a carved wooden horse in the living room. *Opposite below:* The living room is filled with decorative objects from all parts of the world, including Turkish peasant pots and Rajastani chairs.

"MAJAPAHIT AWAKENED"

LOR IN HOTEL SOLO
CENTRAL JAVA, INDONESIA

Set within expansive rice fields on two sides, this two-storey Javanese style small hotel is the place to stay in Solo. The hotel is a celebration of space through calm suavity. Its splendidly peaceful atmosphere is also a result of an inspired use of elements from Javanese culture.

For the first time in his projects in Indonesia, Bensley was able to start cultivating the gardens and sculpting the rice terraces a year before construction of the hotel began.

Bensley has created a very "Javanese" garden, with four sub-gardens of bamboo, palms, bananas, and heat-loving plants. These grounds provide an admirable conti-guity and continuity. The swimming pools overlook a stream, cascading rice fields, and three imposing, seated figures, five metres high, scaled from figures from the heroic Majapahit period of Java. These contemplative

pieces are built from the local stone *batu klatan*.

The design essentially utilizes high walls to screen views. It uses simplicity of construction to achieve gen-erosity of space and light.

Page 146: *Strong silhouettes of the Prambanan Temple located between Solo and Yogyakarta.* **Page 147:** *These three 6-meter high replicas of Majapahit sculpture are made from local white sandstone. More than 50 people took eight months to build it.*

Opposite: *A classic Javanese "pendopo" casts shade on the bubbly spa corner of the main pool. A fire torchere in the pool combines white local sandstone and black andesite.* **Top:** *This Majapahit-style stone panel was designed by Bensley and forms part of the entrance courtyard at the front of the resort.*

From left to right, first row: A pair of bronze monkeys sit at the edge of the children's pool. The view across the swimming pool features another oversized Majapahit- style sculpture. The lifeguard station straddles a courtyard wall. **Second row:** Two serene stone faces. A white Java rhino in white sandstone stands at 1.5 meter high. As descendents of the craftsmen that built great temples like Borobudur, the Javanese retain their highly skilled stone carving talents. **Third row:** The steps down from the red sand court lead to the palm garden. The bronze handrails to the swimming pools are customized with a series of Javanese masks. A complete gamelan greets guests as they arrive at the porte cochere. **Opposite:** Bathed in the early morning light this composition of sculpture looks peacefully across the main courtyards.

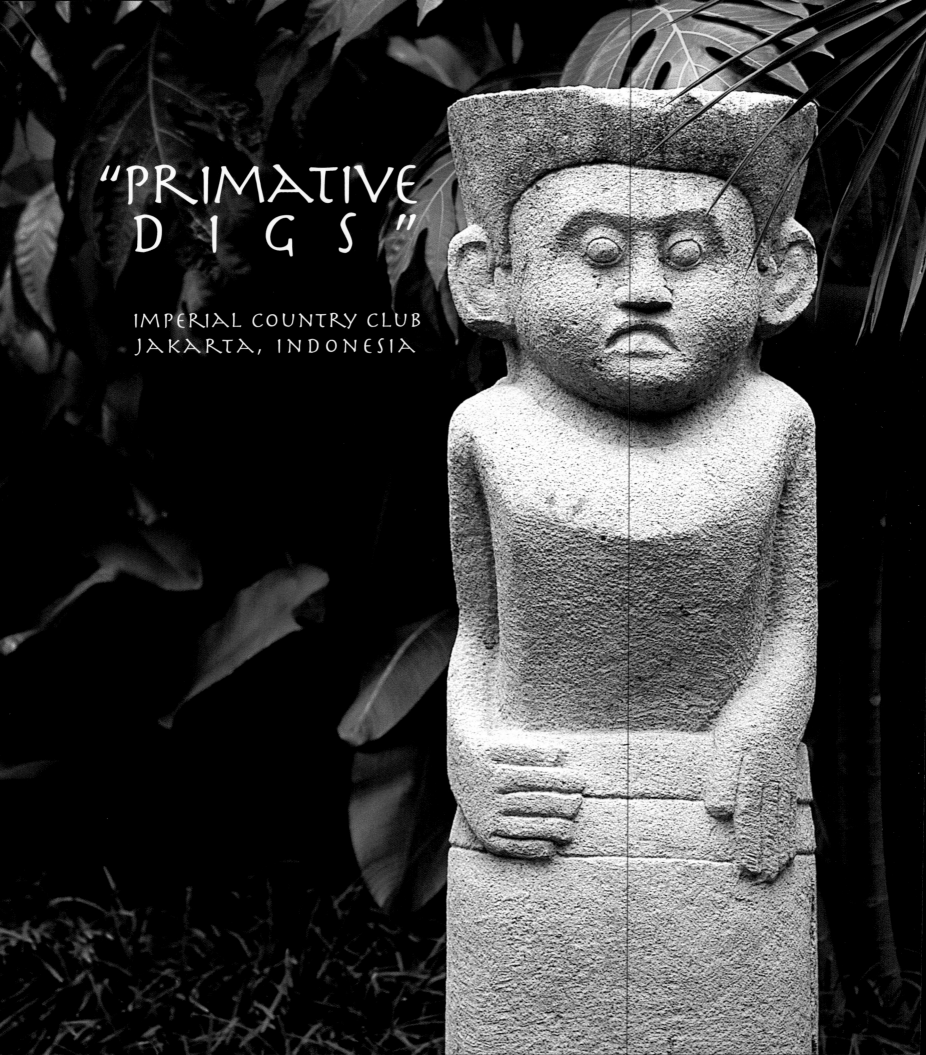

"PRIMATIVE DIGS"

IMPERIAL COUNTRY CLUB
JAKARTA, INDONESIA

Page 153: The focal point of the garden is the "bale" - a pavilion with a raised podium capped by a light roof. **Opposite:** Delightful bamboo water channels spout water from the banana hill's springs. **Right:** Bensley's original sketch for the bamboo water channels. **Below:** Organic vines depicted in ceramics at the bottom of the pool vaguely define lap lanes.

Faced with an increasingly sophisticated clientele, developers of country clubs are forced to look at innovative designs as a selling tool.

Located at Lippo Village, in the suburbs of Jakarta, this is an intensely captivating design. In 1994 Jo Rohn of Lippoland contacted Bensley to see how a newly built country club can renovated to achieve a different ambience. The entire garden was re-designed and within four months, the grounds took on a totally different mood. The interstitial spaces, especially, provide exciting spatial experiences.

The new pool features two tall swim-in cabanas, two four-metre high stone birds perched on the water's surface, and a whole series of giant bamboo water channels originating from a "banana hill" spring and cascading into the main pool. The pool bar is a major departure from the typical design, as it features an African-inspired mud relief wall that soars six meters within the interior of a huge primitive grass hut. The visual impact is immediate.

In its modest way, the Club invigorates and re-engages more of our senses by using visual, tactile and auditory cues in new, refreshing ways. On a relatively small plot of land, the project exudes expansiveness and delight.

Above: Textured surfaces of the secluded entrance to the changing room.
Opposite: The pool bar - with a mixture of "alang alang" and coconut leaves as roof finishes - is complemented by a large standing bird in the middle of the pool.

"A LEAFY RETREAT
IN JAKARTA"

GRAND HYATT JAKARTA, INDONESIA

In early 1995, Bensley was asked to improve the fine garden of the Grand Hyatt Jakarta. Its general manager, Jon Richards, has been most supportive of the designer's effort to quietly and gradually change the existing "look" of the gardens.

Bensley's aim was to create a sense of mystery and surprise, as well as adding new tropical plants for garden enthusiasts. The result is sensorially complex because kinetic movement of the viewer is deliberately harnessed in a well-controlled route. A tall tropical grass music pavilion was built on the swimming pool's edge. The breezeway was also turned into a delightful Javanese-style patio. Twelve columns, taken from traditional Javanese houses, are arranged as an interesting garden display. Sensitive landscaping, combines with found and sculpted artifacts, makes the essentially small space seem much larger.

Dense foliage is employed to provide privacy for the pool. There are also six tennis courts and a jogging track, which have to be landscaped to provide privacy as well. The impact of the tropical idyll is almost immediate.

Page 159: Exuberant planting at the poolside provides privacy for the guests. Above: View of a comfortable "bale" or pavilion filled with forest green and plum-colored pillows and cushions. Top left: Lush landscaping contributes to the overall ambience. Top right: An antique Balinese cabinet. Below left: Influenced by the architecture of Sumba, this thatched music pavilion sits at the edge of the swimming pool. Below right: A soapstone sculpture with hibiscus flowers.

"PARADISE FOUND"

BAAN BOTANICA BANGKOK, THAILAND

Page 163: *The foyer wall has a window punctured through to the dining room. The orange wall is finished with plaster mixed with rice husks, while the sand color is a result of mixing plaster with a particular type of organic fertilizer.* **Top left:** *Night view of the entrance court, with its fountain and gateway.* **Top right:** *All the walls are finished with a unique mixture of mud rice and then dyed in a rusty color obtained from an organic fertilizer.* **Below left:** *K.W. Bensley's room is finished in his favourite color blue.* **Below right:** *This is the real heart of the house. It is where most meals are served. From here, both indoors and outdoors can be appreciated.* **Opposite:** *View of the swimming pool from across a table made by K. W. Bensley under the shade of a custom-made umbrella based on a Burmese design.*

Baan Botanica is the new residence of Bill Bensley, horticulturist Jirachai Rengthong and Bensley's creative father. In many ways, it serves as a laboratory, nursery, workshop, showroom and guest-house.

An existing house was extensively renovated, and an entirely new garden was created. Filled to the brim with antiques, furniture and art works from all corners of the world, the new house is a cross-cultural amalgamation of everything that appeals to the owners.

Baan Botanica is a truly engaging composition of things Thai, Mexican, Moroccan, Burmese, Balinese and Japanese. Its staggering array of objects is displayed to showcase the rich seduction of the handmade. Lush and sumptuous, the house's gallery-like ambience is riveting.

Space folds and enfolds as one moves through the two-storey house, revealing views into gardens, terraces and extending perceptions. Having meticulously resolved the pragmatic concerns, Bensley's inclination for the expressive probity of natural materials, bright colors and exuberant plant forms is obvious. The beautiful gardens, created out of a mix of highly honed sensitivity to tall, large foliage plants and an expressed desire to complement the built structures, evoke different moods and ineffable qualities at different times of the day.

Permeated with light, the spaces reverberate with a certain luminosity and vivacity. Many light sources, used with small fixtures, offer a delightful lighting scheme that is both subtle and vibrant. Thick walls, niches, verandahs and bright colors provide the architectural backdrop, whilst a lushly landscaped pool sits in the midst of the delightful compound. The experience is as much auditory as textural. It is an eloquent reminder of the delight of the intense interaction between landscape, architecture and art.

Top right: The house employs a series of old windows inserted into solid walls. Bensley has installed Indian palace windows from Rajastan, wooden marshabeyas from Iran, turn-of-the-century windows from Burma and this Balinese window with a frame designed by Jirachai Rengthong in the dining room. ***Below:*** *A quiet corner in the living room. Close-up of a 1920s (Art Deco) version of the traditional Thai "spirit house".*

Opposite: The "elephant room" opens out to the verandahs and gardens on both sides.

Opposite: *This guest room is furnished as white on stressed white and is ethinc and contemporary at the same time.* **Top left:** *Master bedroom of the Baan Botanica.* **Top right:** *The verandah doubles as a dining room in the cool season.* **Below left:** *Layers of doors and windows, some 300 years old, are the dominant themes of the house.* **Below right:** *A Mexican-style fountain, located at the entry gate, has black polished granite and beige sandstone in a harlequin pattern.*

Top left: *The house is about moods, ambience and lights.* **Top right:** *View of the master bedroom where a 1930's Burmese safe deposit box is used as the headboard.* **Below left:** *View of the master bedroom.* **Below right:** *The evocative lighting helps to imbue the house with a highly atmospheric quality.* **Opposite:** *The master bedroom is paneled with the walls of an old Thai house. Banana flowers sit on top of a 18th century Chinese medicine cabinet while fresh seeds from a fishtail palm (Caryota mitas) hang from the wall. The "hanuman" monkey figure is an architectural bracket from a northern Thai temple.*

CONCEIVING
PARADISE

1

2

3

The studios of Bensley and Bunnag have consistently, and without any sense of complacency, produced a vigorous stream of projects.

New works, exhibiting the signature dose of craft, humor and warmth will certainly be as tantalizing and memorable, far from the staid, vapid structures of most resorts. Marked by an elegance of fabrication and a concern for place, the next wave of evolving projects will further validate - and in dramatic fashion - this highly tactile strand of architecture.

As Bensley himself admits: " There is a lifetime of work to be done in Asia. I want the common guy to get a buzz from our gardens. I really don't think we have done any really good garden yet. I would like to get to that stage. This attitude, hopefully, will keep me "alive" for a long time." It is through this profoundly simple acknowledgement that both designers can create works that exhibit tender understanding and appreciation of the phenomenal world.

As the two studios struggle to find content and innovation in the usual meager briefs of most resorts, the most challenging task is to continually interpret the intangibles of host cultures into tangible forms and landscapes. Aside from honed architectural strategies for the siting of structures, linkage and animation of constructional components, a refined reading of traditional forms with a sensuous artistic practice is critical.

We need to contaminate the new space of the vernacular and to relocate it in the evolving cultural landscape. This indicates a need to venture beyond insular and exclusive tendencies towards a more global and inclusive architecture. As critic Sola-Morales observes: "Our concern here is not with the use of stylistic codes that render a building recognizable as a particular instance of a common language, but with the search, in each case and for each work, for the presence and the manifestation that are inherently proper to it."

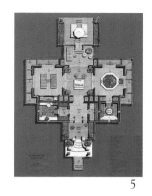

4

5

6

In today's fragmented, post-capitalist society, buildings around the world are rarely produced by craftsmen. Traditional forms no longer represent how buildings are now being constructed. The logic of construction of traditional architecture was visually apparent to everyone — the architecture represented directly the materials used and the method of construction employed. It incorporated technical and significative norms at the same time. These "transparent" technologies are gradually being displaced by the evolution of material science. Quality is not judged by the skill of fabrication, but more the skill of installation. Workmanship is valued above craftsmanship.

Figuration in architecture hence becomes less to do with response to materials and more to do with the associative attributes of particular shapes and forms. For example, the construction cost devoted to structure today has decreased from 80% to 20%, while that for the building's skin has increased to 12%. There is hence a cultural devaluation of the tectonic.

The question remains - how do we seek out continuities with local conditions and to be profoundly evocative of tradition. In an incisive essay "The Interpretative Imperative" in Harvard Design Magazine (Fall 1997), Sandy Isenstadt argues that "symbolic persistence in architecture, then, is less a matter of finding a universally understood symbol than of continuing to inspire interpretation. The interpretative imperative is architecture's contribution to remembrance in an age of perfectible memory."

(1): A drawing by Bunnag for a competition for the design of Amanjiwo. It is based on the concept of the Javanese "pendolpo", where the idea is not to overshadow Borobudur. (2): Close-up of the palatial lobby ceiling at Novotel Lombok. (3): Drawing for the kids' club at St. Geran Hotel in the east coast of Mauritius. (4): Interior section of a guestroom at the unbuilt Banyu Wedang in northern Bali. (5): Plan of the floating spa pavilion at Spa Bay, Pangkor Laut, Malaysia. (6): Plan of the pineapple garden at Banyu Wedang, the focal point of a series of Dutch-colonial villas. They have crescent-designed facades, with gardens located behind. **Below:** *Rendered view of the public spaces at Sofitel Denarau Island Resort in Fiji.*

"FIT FOR A PHAROAH"
OBEROI TABA, EGYPT

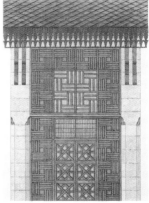

In this intense, hot and dry landscape of Taba, Egypt, one finds visual relief only in the cool depths of the Red Sea. There is not a single tree in the entire site, which slopes towards the beach, where the Gulf of Aquba joins the Red Sea.

This collaborative effort by Bunnag and Bensley is designed such that every guest has clear views of the sea whilst swimming in the privacy of his private 15-metre lap pool. There are altogether 80 villas. Each villa has tall pivoted timber doors leading to the bedroom, bathroom, walk-in closet and outdoor bath pavilion. Sunlight enters the room through skylights made of 2m deep truncated cones. At the top of the skylights are colored glass. These villas are connected by beautiful, narrow alleys in a Medina-like network of routes.

The strongest image of the development is perhaps the restaurant block, which is composed of 14 local sandstone columns forming two colonnades. Each of these column has a diameter of 4 m and a height of 15 m. The colonnades are aligned in an axial arrangement with the gap between two mountain ranges.

Built on a very steep site, the project is a massive challenge. As Bensley puts it: "This project tests our adaptability to work, once again, in a completely unfamiliar environment with a completely new set of architectural language to learn."

Top: *Egyptian architecture.*
Middle: *Detail of a traditional Egyptian window, "marshal beya", which is a type of privacy screen. The original drawing measures 0.60 x 0.45 m.*
Left: *Plan illustration of the terraced guest room. The original drawing mesures 1.00 x 0.70 m.*

Opposite: *The restaurant features a series of columns, with a canvas canopy hanging above the restaurant. It is centered on an important natural geographical axis, where the Red Sea and the land masses of Saudi Arabia and Egypt meet. The original drawing measures 0.70 x 0.80 m.*

Lawn
and
Breakfast
Area

Bathtub Pavilion

Agava Court

fountain

love seat niche

ing l

Section of the terraced guestrooms. Level differences between the units are almost 5 metres. Buffer landscape zones between the units provide complete privacy in all the outdoor private spaces. The original drawing measures 1.40 x 0.90 m.

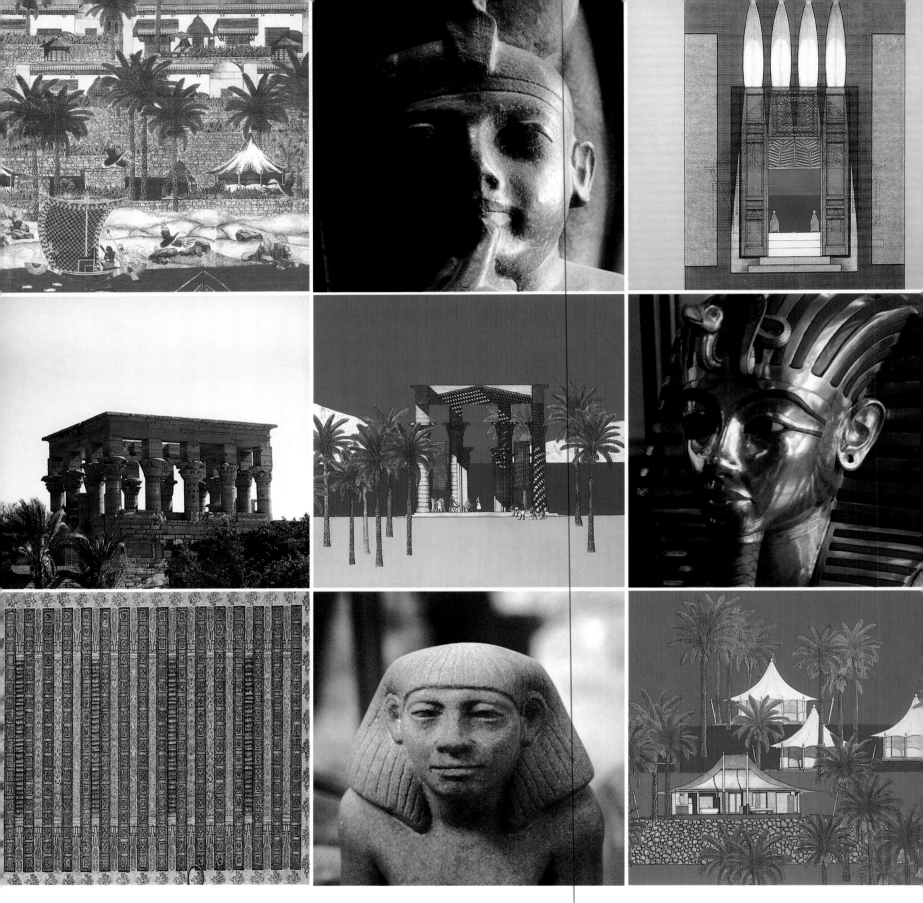

From left to right, first row: *Guestroom elevation from the sea. An Egyptian face mask. Section of the connector foyer, between the bedroom and the bathroom. The original drawing measures 0.61 x 1.30 m.* **Second row:** *Lobby at the top of the hill, the highest position on the site. It looks down on the circulation corridor. The original drawing measures 0.80 x 0.80 m. Section showing the play of light and shadow. An Egytian mask is perhaps the poignant symbol of Egyptian culture.* **Third row:** *Ceiling detail of the bedroom. Another Egyptian artwork. Elevational view of the twelve tents, surrounded by an oasis-like swimming pool.*

180

From left to right, first row: *An Egyptian mask. Elevational view of the twelve tents. Stone carvings depiciting symbolic animals and birds.* **Second row:** *A concept drawing depicting the land masses of Egpyt, Saudi Arabia and the Red Sea, together with a private pavilion and a swimming pool. The original drawing measures 0.52 x 0.76 m. An Egyptian wall-relief window opening.* **Third row:** *Views of the powerful land masses and the sea. An elevation view of the columns. Close-up of columns.*

"BASALT BOULDERS"
OBEROI MAURITIUS AT BALACLAVA

Mauritius has also been conventionally touted as a wonderful tourist destination. The Oberoi seeks to create a refreshing addition to the local resort scene. The design for the resort has evolved considerably since the project started in 1996.

Faced with challenging budget constraints, Bunnag and Bensley have to rectify an earlier proposal by achieving 95% sea views from the rooms. This did not come easy as the flat site is reconstructed into one with undulating contours. Throughout the site, some 30,000 cubic metres of basalt boulders, some as large as a car, have to be excavated and relocated on the very flat site. In addition, many of these excavated boulders are stacked to create beautiful boundary walls and retaining walls for the numerous sunken gardens. The crevices of these basalt walls are further filled with earth, allowing interesting "mini-gardens" to be created on the walls' vertical surfaces.

Top: The famous Amazon lily pool at pamplemouse botanical garden. **Below:** *Masterplan for Oberoi Mauritius. It has 48 typical units, 15 grand suites with pools, 9 grand suites without pools and 2 deluxe suites. The original drawing measures 1.66 x 2.44 m.*

Opposite Top: An elevation showing the water features. The original drawing measures 0.87 x 1.11 m. **Opposite below:** *Front elevation of the grand suites.*

"MUMBAI MIX "

MARRIOTT MUMBAI JUHU BEACH , INDIA

Located at the outskirts of Mumbai, Juhu Beach is becoming the new business centre just minutes from the Mumbai Airport. With interiors designed by Hirsh Bedner, this 300-room hotel is an opulent addition to the Mumbai hotel scene.

Bensley designed a tropical seaside garden that features four pools - a 40 x 30 m lap pool, a cold dip pool, a children's pool featuring an alligator slide, and a naturalistic waterfall pool. These gardens are accented with a series of custom-designed Indian stone sculptures crafted by the skilled artisans of Rajasthan.

The main landscape preoccupations are with space and framing of vistas. The subtle play of water and landscape asserts an air of meditative power.

The resort will open in 2002.

Opposite: *The masterplan of the beach side gardens. The original drawing measures 2.67 m.*
Below right: *Section of the lap pool. The original drawing measures 0.53 x 0.86 m.*

"THE NEW ANCIENT"

UDAIVILAS, UDAIPUR, INDIA

In the heart of Rajasthan, and on the banks of the famous Pichola Lake (where the James Bond movie "Octopussy" was filmed), the Oberoi group is building a hotel in the grand tradition of the Mawar style. The architect Nimish Patel specializes in traditional Rajasthani architecture and vernacular building methods. Bensley is involved in the design of the gardens. He has responded to the sense of place with great grace.

There will be about 90 rooms. Many of them, each with a private pool, overlook the Lake Palace. The interiors are by H. L. Lim & Associates. All the sculptural elements in the gardens are designed along the distinctive aesthetic lines of the Mewar, one of the many kingdoms of ancient India.

In order to make the presentation drawings captivating and local in essence, Bensley's studio artists borrowed the traditional Mogul miniaturized style of painting. Using false flat perspectives, a riot of colors accented by some 300 sheets of gold gilt, and fanciful ancient symbols for trees and human figures, a rich, dream-like mood was depicted in grand evocative style. Some 45 metres of drawings were created to depict the intended moods and design intentions. The resort will open in 2002.

Below: Masterplan showing the lakeside and the courtyards. The original drawing measures 1.55 x 1.97 m. ***Opposite:*** *"Courtyard of hospitality" - where a beautiful, ornate pavilion is located. The series of drawings are executed in traditional Mughal style with distorted perspectives. The original drawing measures 0.90 x 0.90 m.*

Top left: *Elevation of the lobby as seen from Udaipur Lake, with the red-earth mountains in the background. The original drawing measures 1.50 x 1.00 m.* **Below left:** *Approach towards the entrance courtyard from the lake. The original drawing measures 0.77 x 1.37 m.* **Opposite top:** *Another variation of the entrance courtyard showing the pervasive use of black and white marble. The original drawing measures 1.12 x 0.87 m.* **Opposite below from left to right:** *Views of the City Palace hotel in Udaipur.*

"OF SPIRITUALITY, SPRINGS AND SPAS"

SHISEIDO SPA ,BALI, INDONESIA

Set in Sayang, near the artistic heart of Ubud in Bali, this Spa boasts of a tantalizingly escapist sanctuary. Its greatest asset is probably the fact that it enjoys an extraordinarily stunning site that overlooks the Sayang Gorge. Many sacred sanctuaries had been built along its steep banks. Surrounded by verdant rice terraces, the presence of the green essence of the landscape is pervasive. Appropriately, the Spa has a grandeur expressly designed for the majesty of the setting. A strong sense of horizontality is achieved by the use of massive stone walls that cut across the steep contours.

The Spa consists of individual villas built in traditional Balinese style with outdoor showers, open-sided pavilions, private courtyards and landscaped gardens. In this respect, the typology adopted is one that that has already been well established by significant Balinese precedents. However a cluster of villas solely dedicated to spa facilities is the first of its kind.

Enclosed behind dramatic high walls, these restful villas assert their presence quietly and with grace. They have their own intimate swimming pools overlooking spectacular rice terraces and emerald forests that shimmer with a particular radiance in the late light of the evening.

Water gardens will have water pumped up from the Ayung River. These will be found throughout the grounds. There are also dozens of water features of every descriptions to both delight and surprise. The design earnestly seeks serenity in tactile materials, expressing by design their essential nature.

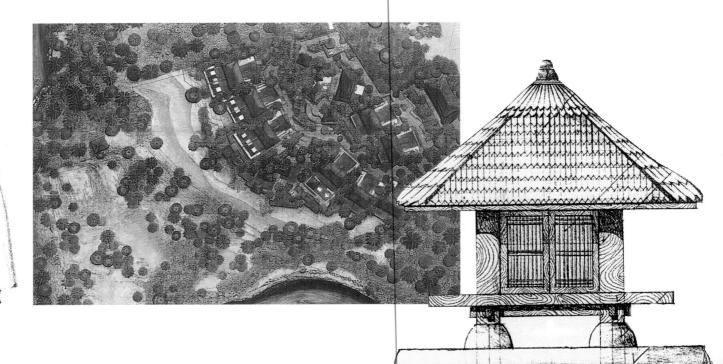

192

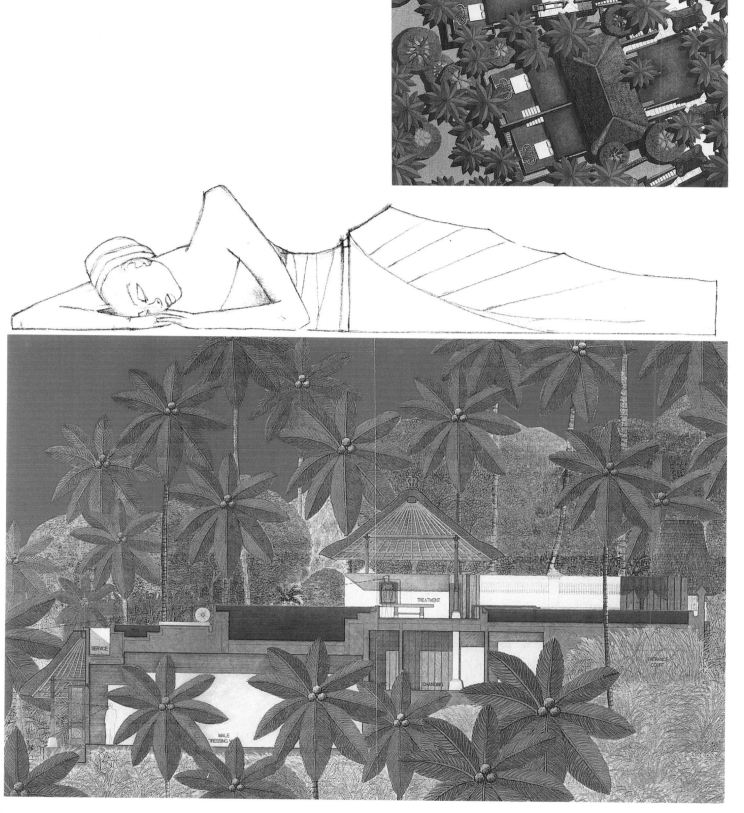

Opposite below middle: *Masterplan showing the steep site and its relationship to the Ayung River. The original drawing measures 0.53 x 0.76 m.* **Above**: *Plan of the massage pavilion with a lily pond at one side and a private dip pool on the other. The original drawing measures 0.53 x 0.76 m.* **Below:** *Section of a private unit. The original drawing measures 0.50 x 0.84 m.*

"TWIST OF ZEN"

TANJUNG RHU RESORT
LANGKAWI, MALAYSIA

This is a 150-room resort on the island of Langkawi, with its own 2 km long beach. It offers two types of accommodation - the beach villa and the "Melaluca" suite. Each of the former is about 150 sq. m whilst the latter occupies about 50 sq. m. These bungalows are very spacious.

There is a meditative, Zen-like quality to the design of the bathrooms. Wooden bathtubs, sliding panels and huge 12m long patios all add to the luxury of the bath design. From the exercise room in the bath, guests will be able to see the majestic limestone cliffs in the distance. The 4.5m high door to the private shower garden is designed to capture these exhilarating views.

The gardens consist of a series of long, vignettes where long walls of stacked boulder walls are juxtaposed with architectural "rooms" of trees. There are also more than twenty private dip pools and another five common pools dotted throughout the property.

Top left: *Sectional elevation of the beach villa showing its relationship to the white limestone cliffs and dense jungle foliage in the background. The original drawing measures 0.95x 0.84 m.* **Top right:** *Drawing showing the public spaces and the restaurants. The original drawing measures 0.50 x 0.84 m.* **Below left:** *Plan of the beachside villa. The original drawing measures 0.66 x 0.56 m.* **Below right:** *Sectional elevation of the beach villa showing its relationship to the white limestone cliffs and dense jungle foliage in the background. The original drawing measures 0.60 x 0.84m.*

"A DESERT OASIS"

OBEROI JAISELMER INDIA

Jaiselmer is a World Heritage site

and is located in one of the most remote regions of India. It has spectacular scenery, but is unbearably hot for 9 months of the year.

The town is famous because it is the site of an ancient fortress that sits atop an outcrop of golden-orange Jaiselmer rocks. Within the walls of the fortress, one finds beautiful architectural gems in the form of exquisite houses. Every element of these houses is built from Jaiselmer stones. The house are adorned with beautiful carvings, executed with such fine artisanry that the stonework resembles elaborate woodcraft.

The intimate resort is located some 5 km away from this exquisite historical setting. It will attempt to capture the character of this setting by using thousands of craftsmen to produce structures and artworks out of the indigeneous stones. There are about 45 keys and twelve free-standing tents clustered around an oasis-like swimming pool.

Opposite top: *A comfortable jute bed and a cosmetic closet found in a typical Rajastani house.* **Opposite below:** *Masterplan of the resort. The original drawing measures 0.90 x 1.70 m.* **Top:** *Sectional view of the guestroom showing a raised jacuzzi pavilion that overlooks miles of red hot sand. The drawing technique uses colored mylar with dozens of orange and terracotta markers in order to capture the severe heat of the place. The original drawing measures 0.85 x 0.77 m.* **Below left:** *Elevation of the entrance gazebo. The original drawing measures 0.40 x 0.60 m.* **Below middle:** *The pavilion is influenced by local reservoir architecture. The original drawing measures 0.40 x 0.60 m.* **Below right:** *Interior elevational view of the entrance courtyard wall. The original drawing measures 0.40 x 0.45 m.*

NOVOTEL BALI

After the resounding success of Novotel Benoa, the owner decided to build a new extension to add more keys to the hotel. A piece of land adjacent to the hotel was acquired, and both Bunnag and Bensley extended the same design language, albeit in a more celebratory manner. The main focus was on water, and thick verdant landscape to create a sense of space.

Top: *Beach view at Bali Benoa.*
Below: *Masterplan of the new extension. The original drawing measures 0.99 x 0.84 m.*

Above: *Beachscape with the cabanas forming an interesting silhouette. The original drawing measures 0.60 x 0.84 m.*
Below left: *Elevational view of private cabanas*

and pool pockets. The original drawing measures 0.59 x 0.84 m.
Below right: *Sectional view of the new extension. The original drawing measures 0.59 x 0.84 m.*

TAIB RESIDENCE

The Taib Residence is a large estate of pavilions designed to accommodate a large family, together with a host of guest residences. It is designed to fit into a prime double-lot site at the Le Meridien's Tanah Lot enclave. The site slopes dramatically towards the sea, and the design makes the most of this topography. Bensley has designed rice terraces at the edge of the adjacent golf course. Bunnag designed the dramatic architecture of interconnected pavilions.

Below: *Site plan of the house. The original drawing measures 0.82 x 0.56m.* **Opposite top:** *Elevational view from the adjacent rice terraces and golf course. The original drawing measures 0.53 x 0.75m.* **Opposite below left:** *A typical "paras" stone house temple.* **Opposite below right:** *Elevation of the pavilions. The original drawing measures 0.53 x 0.75m.*

THE STUDIOS

Both Bensley and Bunnag have created a memorable series of places and experiences, imbued with brilliant flashes of wit, passion and painstakingly crafted details. In their relentless quest for beauty in tropical gardens and architecture, both attempt to create environments of ambivalent qualities and often, refreshing vitality.

The two studios and their staff have worked marvellously well as separate entities where necessary, and as cohesive partners in collaborative projects. However, the pervasive quality is one of meticulous zeal and much delicacy.

In order to introduce tactile gratification and a precious sense of the tectonic in the built environment, the same qualities must necessarily be present at the concept stage. Architecture is essentially an anachronistic form of art, where speed and ephemerality have nothing to do with its production. The design process, in striving for an innovative formal vocabulary, hence takes time and passion. This is in contrast to today's age in which speed and cybernetic disposability are the order of the day.

Some critics call such design process obsessively elaborate and perhaps even frivolous. Indeed, they are invariably multi-faceted and at the same time, time-consuming. But in the search for a new vocabulary of lyricism based on an empathy for the landscape, this is inevitable. Decisions have to be made slowly, because the struggles to achieve a sense of unity and invention have to be comprehensive. The simple message appears to be that architecture and landscape are to be seen as the results of the elemental needs of man and the natural materials around us.

Since the tendency is to prioritise visual and formal qualities, crisp drawings are produced with exquisite care and elaborate details. Drawings and paintings provide the means that liberate individual energies. They are admirably undogmatic moves, and they form active parts of the design process. Jeff Wall, an artist who has established himself as probably the most important artist using photography working today, argues : "Depiction is an act of construction; it brings the referent into being. All the fine arts share this characteristic, regardless of other differences."

Most importantly, the act of engendering, unfolding and participating in emergent realities must be poignant and satisfying. In both studios, the drawings are reflective of this capacity to be deeply intense, and in the process, **have fun too.**

"The commitment of architects to their freedom in whatever design circumstances confirms their responsibility and constitutes their pleasure: this freedom is inevitable and real, preventing the temptation of determinism."

Rafael Moneo

"By adorning anything, be it alive or inanimate, I bestow upon it the right of individual life. By making it the center of relations that pertain to it alone, I elevate it to the rank of a person."

Gottried Semper

My most rewarding professional experience is the sharing of a studio in Bangkok with Bill. We both maintain at least 8-10 artists in our practices. They produce wonderful stimulation and support to our work, as well as enhancing my belief that architecture alone is not enough. It is only with landscape, sculpture and painting that architecture starts to sing.

With a 10 meters long central table in our studio, our landscape architects, architects, artists, driver and maid enjoy producing wonderful and colorful drawings which make all of us feel good. This is the core of our studio. We usually produce our drawings at a scale of 1:50 for architecture and landscape and 1:200 or 1:500 for site plans. Our eyes have become familiar with these scales. We know well when somebody has drawn the wrong size... be it a heliconia leaf or a buggy path.

All drawings must have shadows and be presented as realistic and precise as possible.

It has been an ongoing joke that every architect in our office must always hold a scale in his hand and keep a measuring tape in his pocket, otherwise Mr. Bunnag will get upset.

It is always my intention to train our architects to measure every hotel room they stay and places we visit. I think that it is the only way we can be precise about our decisions.

The most challenging (and Bill & I found it at the same time great fun) task is to charge our image and imagination in mathematical terms. All our imagination then become "measurable". Mathematics must always test our decision and our precision, therefore challenging our intentions about form.

A person full of visual memories and imagination, Bill is the greatest contemporary artist I know. He grows with things around him. He extends an idea and image with precision and clarity. He not only always makes me think clearer when I am not clear but also extends any idea and imagination further to richer visual fantasies. I always feel that we see similar concepts when we decide on images and imagination, perhaps because we often travel and wander through many parts of the world together, from Fez to Fiji.

One of his greatest asset is his memory, both visual and non-visual. It was great fun when both of us sit together designing, recalling past images we have seen together. We combine, recompose, and add. What we have seen flows together without fear of borrowing.

Bill opens doors of varieties of form for me. I studied architecture in the late 60's when my extensive travelling then was focused on Le Corbusier and Khan. My 8 months' experience of overland trip from Germany to Nepal with my best friend - a great designer Manop Phakinsri - was my most memorable. That experience has deeply diverted my imagination about form. Le Cobusier and Kahn, and their principles of architecture, remain guiding posts in my decisions till today.

Both Bill and I love to sit in front of 2-3 computer screens at the same time and direct computer draftsmen to draw. Somehow, I find this very enjoyable and extremely productive, although neither of us know how to switch the computer "on"!

I will always believe that there is nothing accidental about making architecture and beauty. Architecture is about our precise decisions, and what we want them to be.

Lek Bunnag

LIST OF PROJECTS

Thailand; Regent/Four Seasons, Chiang Mai Mai, fax (66 53) 298 189, e-mail reservations @fourseasons.com*, Sheraton Grande Sukhumvit, Bangkok,fax (66 2) 653 0400, e-mail grande_sukhumvit@sheraton.com, Marriott Royal Garden Riverside, Bangkok,fax (66 2) 476 1120, e-mail MARRIOTTRGR@minornet.com, Royal Garden Village, Hua Hin .fax (66 32) 520259-60, e-mail royalgarden-vhh@minornet.com*, Royal Garden Resort, Hua Hin, fax (66 32) 512 422, e-mail royalgardenrhh@minor-net.com, Pan Pacific Hotel, Bangkok, fax (66 2) 632 9163, e-mail rsvn@panpacbkk.com, Four Seasons Phuket*, Marriott Phuket. Phuket, Indonesia; Sheraton Towers, Jakarta, Sheraton Senggigi Beach Resort, Lombok, fax (62 270) 693 135, e-mail Sheraton@indo.net.id,*, Lor In Hotel, Solo Central Java,fax (62 271) 724123, e-mail lorin@indo.net.id, Sheraton Lagoon, Bali, extension project,fax (62 361) 771 326, E-mail erhard_hotter@sheraton.com*, Sheraton Surabaya, East Java, fax (62 31) 546 7000, e-mail Sheraton.rad.net.id, Sheraton Inn Temika, Irian Jaya, fax (62 901) 394951, e-mail Urs_Klee@fmi.com, Conrad Hilton Hotel, Jakarta, Marriott Hotel, Jakarta, Grand Hyatt, Jakarta - Renovations, fax (62 21) 3906426, e-mail GHYAT-TJK@CBN.Net.Id, Grand Hyatt Residences, Jakarta , Bali Hyatt; The beach swimming pool complex fax (62 361) 287693, Westin Hotel, Jakarta, Four Seasons Residences, Jakarta, Taman Niaga Country and Golf Club, Jakarta , Bali Imperial Hotel, Legian Beach, Bali, Novotel, Tanjung Benoa, Bali fax (62 361) 772 237, e-mail novotelbali@bali-paradis.com*, Novotel Hotel, Bogor, West Java fax (62 251) 271 333, e-mail novobogor@indo.net.id*, Novotel Hotel, Kute Beach, Lombok, fax (62 370) 653 555, e-mail hotel@novotel-lombok.com*, Carita Bay Resort, Jakarta , Imperial Country Club, Jakarta, Shiseido Spa, Ubud, Indonesia*, Malaysia; Tanjung Rhu Langkawi, Malaysia*, Sofitel Johor Barhu, Johor, Malaysia*, Bukit Bayu Club House, Kuala Lumpur, Malaysia*, PangkLaut Resort, Malaysia,fax (605) 699 1200, e-mail plr@po.jaring.my*, Tanjungjara Hotel, Kuantan, Malaysia – Renovations, fax (609) 845 1200, e-mail tjara@po.jaring.my*, India; Marriott Mumbai at Juhu Beach, Mumbai, India, The Rajvilas, Jaipur, India,fax (91 141) 640 202, e-mail sdatta@rajvilas.com, - An Oberoi Hotel, Udai Vilas, Udaipur, India, Oberoi Jaisalmer, India, Oberoi Agra, India, Kenilworth Beach Resort, Goa, India, Holiday Inn Mumbai, Juhu Beach, India, Worldwide; Four Seasons Resort,Hualalai at Historic Kalupulahu, Hawaii, U.S.A. fax (808) 325 8053, Grand Hyatt Istanbul, Turkey , fax (90 212) 225 7007, East 21st Hotel, Tokyo Bay, Kandawgyi Palace Hotel, Yangon, Myanmar,fax (95 1) 242 776, e-mail kandawgyi@baiyoke.co.th*, Oberoi Mauritius*, Westin Hotel, Taipei, Taiwan, St. Geran Resort, Mauritius, Oberoi Taba, Cairo*, Yak & Yeti Hotel, Kathmandu, Nepal, fax (997 1) 227 782, e-mail reservation@yakandyeti.com., Novotel Fiji, Fiji* All of the above projects are in the Bensley Design Studios portfolio. *Means included in Bunnag Architects portfolio.

Bensley Design Studios and Bunnag Architects contacts;167/1 Soi Ekamai 5 Sukumvit 63 Road Bangkok 10110, Thailand Telephone; 66 2 711 4330 Fax; 66 2 398 5562 e-mail:bensley@mozart.inet.co.th or bunnag@loxinfo.co.th Visit their website at www..bensley.com

PHOTO CREDITS

Unless otherwise stated, all photographs
in the book are taken by Bill Bensley.

BIBLIOGRAPHY

William Howard Adams, Grounds for Change – Major
Gardens of the Twentieth Century, Bulfinch Press, 1993
Gaston Bachelard, The Poetics of Space, Beacon Press,
Boston.
Jean-Louis Bourgeois, Spectacular Vernacular, Aperture
Foundation, Inc., New York, 1989
Kendall H. Brown, Japanese-Style Gardens of the Pacific
West Coast, Rizzoli, New York, 1999
Petra Carroll, "Thailand's Regent Chiang Mai" in
Architectural Digest, September 1995
Sylvia Crowe, Sheila Haywood, The Gardens of Mughul
India, Vikas Publishing House Pte Ltd, Delhi, 1973
Michael Dunworth, "Jungle Booking" in Belle, Dec/Jan
1996
Jane Edwards, Asian Elements, Conran Octopus
Ltd,London, 1999
Kenneth Frampton, Studies in Tectonic Culture, MIT
Press, 1995
Jan Fontein, The Sculpture of Indonesia, National
Gallery of Art, Washington, 1990
Carol Lutfy, "Rajvilas Rising" in Architectural Digest,
August 1998
Carol Lutfy, "Reinterpreting Traditions For A New
Indonesian Resort" in Architectural Digest, December
1999

Juhani Pallasmaa, "An Architecture of the Seven
Senses" in Questions of Perception, A+U
Architecture and Urbanism, July 1994 Special Issue.
Christian Norberg-Schulz, Genius Loci: Towards a
Phenomenology of Architecture, New York: Rizzoli
International Publications, Inc., 1980.
David Stevens, Ursula Buchan, The Conran Octopus
Garden Book, Conran Octopus Ltd, London, 1994
Tan Hock Beng, Tropical Architecture and Interiors,
Page One Publishing Pte Ltd, Singapore, 1994
Tan Hock Beng, Tropical Resorts, Page One
Publishing Pte Ltd, Singapore, 1995
Tan Hock Beng, Tropical Retreats, Page One
Publishing Pte Ltd, Singapore, 1996
Tan Hock Beng, William Lim, Contemporary
Vernacular, Select Books Pte Ltd, Singapore, 1998.
Jun'ichiro Tanizaki, In Praise of Shadows , translated
by Thomas J. Harper and Edward G. Seidensticker,
Charles E. Tuttle Company, Inc, Tokyo, 1990.
William Warren, Thai Garden Style, Periplus
Editions (HK) Ltd, Singapore, 1996
Jennifer Westwood, ed., The Atlas of Mysterious
Places, Weidenfeld & Nicolson, New York, 1987
Herbert YPMA, Hip Hotels – City, Thames and
Hudson, New York, 1999

THANK YOU!

ACKNOWLEDGMENTS

Making this book has been a very enjoyable process, and this is partially due to the subject and partially because the two key persons involved in the book are engaging, stimulating and most importantly, fun to work with. It is an exhilarating project and there are many people without whom it would never have been completed. I would like to specifically thank two key persons involved in the book. The input of two of the main protagonists of the book - Bill Bensley and Lek Bunnag - has been tremendous They have passionately shared their time and profound knowledge of the region with me. These they have done with humour, patience and much energy. Their creative spirit, insight and friendship have been a revelation and a great inspiration.

I also owe special gratitude to my publisher, Mark Tan, who once again initiated the early ideas, as well as Violet Tan for her abilities to co-ordinate so many different things at the same time. The book designer Robbie Gilchrist has also done a wonderful job in bringing his singular vision to the project, giving a refreshing and visually exciting form to the many beautiful images, all within a relatively short period of time. Bensley Design Studios and K C Sin of Maxim Design have also form the creative spine in fleshing out the final stages of the layout.

I also wish to thank Louisa Bunnag and Jirachai Rengthong for their unflagging support and kind hospitality.

All the members of the Bensley Design Studios and Bunnag Architects in Bangkok also deserves great appreciation for their invaluable contributions. They have helped immeasurably in putting together the book. They include Brian Sherman for his support, Khemvadee "Quant" Paopanlerd for her exquisite drawings, as well as Keng for her administrative support.

For reading and responding to various parts of the book, and for their honest opinions, I owe tremendous debts to many friends who have contributed in unchartable ways. In particular, I wish to thank Robert Powell, Chua Beng Huat, Kathleen Davidson, Eddy Koh and Clara Pong.

Among these, particular credit should be accorded to Germaine Koh and Chang Ai Hua. I also wish to thank my colleagues in the office, especially Anthea Gan, Ho Tzu Yin, Alvin Foo, Carol Yeo and Millie Cher, for making it easier for me to leave the office on many trips.

Most of all, my gratitude goes to my family : Maria, Brent and Gale. They have been yet again the powerful leading forces behind its completion.

Tan Hock Beng
Singapore, 2000